The Father we never knew

The unbinding of the Lazarus Church by the restoration of the gospel

Phelim Doherty

Copyright © 2017 Phelim Doherty.

All rights reserved. No part of this book may be used or reproduced by any means, graphic, electronic, or mechanical, including photocopying, recording, taping or by any information storage retrieval system without the written permission of the author except in the case of brief quotations embodied in critical articles and reviews.

This book is a work of non-fiction. Unless otherwise noted, the author and the publisher make no explicit guarantees as to the accuracy of the information contained in this book and in some cases, names of people and places have been altered to protect their privacy.

WestBow Press books may be ordered through booksellers or by contacting:

WestBow Press
A Division of Thomas Nelson & Zondervan
1663 Liberty Drive
Bloomington, IN 47403
www.westbowpress.com
1 (866) 928-1240

Because of the dynamic nature of the Internet, any web addresses or links contained in this book may have changed since publication and may no longer be valid. The views expressed in this work are solely those of the author and do not necessarily reflect the views of the publisher, and the publisher hereby disclaims any responsibility for them.

Any people depicted in stock imagery provided by Thinkstock are models, and such images are being used for illustrative purposes only. Certain stock imagery © Thinkstock.

ISBN: 978-1-5127-7382-8 (sc)
ISBN: 978-1-5127-7383-5 (hc)
ISBN: 978-1-5127-7381-1 (e)

Library of Congress Control Number: 2017901320

Print information available on the last page.

WestBow Press rev. date: 2/27/2017

Scripture quotations marked NKJV are taken from the New King James Version. Copyright 1982 by Thomas Nelson, Inc. Used by permission. All rights reserved.

Scripture quotations marked NLT are taken from the Holy Bible, New Living Translation, copyright 1996, 2004, 2007. Used by permission of Tyndale House Publishers, Inc. Carol Stream, Illinois 60188. All rights reserved.

Scripture quotations marked KJV are from the Holy Bible, King James Version (Authorized Version). First published in 1611. Quoted from the KJV Classic Reference Bible, Copyright 1983 by The Zondervan Corporation.

Scripture quotations marked NIV are taken from the Holy Bible, New International Version. NIV. Copyright 1973, 1978, 1984 by International Bible Society. Used by permission of Zondervan. All rights reserved.

Scripture quotations marked AMP are from The Amplified Bible, Old Testament copyright 1965, 1987 by the Zondervan Corporation. The Amplified Bible, New Testament copyright 1954, 1958, 1987 by The Lockman Foundation. Used by permission. All rights reserved.

Scripture quotations marked NASB are taken from the New American Standard Bible, Copyright 1960, 1962, 1963, 1968, 1971, 1972, 1973, 1975, 1977, 1995 by The Lockman Foundation. Used by permission.

Scripture quotations marked MSG are taken from THE MESSAGE. Copyright 1993, 1994, 1995, 1996, 2000, 2001, 2002, 2003 by Eugene H. Peterson. Used by permission of NavPress Publishing Group.

Strong's Exhaustive Concordance: New American Standard Bible. Updated ed. La Habra: Lockman Foundation, 1995. http://www.biblestudytools.com/concordances/strongs-exhaustive-concordance/.

Contents

Dedication ix
Introduction xi

Chapter 1	The unveiling of the church 1
Chapter 2	Beginning in rest 9
Chapter 3	The Father we never knew 14
Chapter 4	The apostolic foundation 22
Chapter 5	Grace—His divine influence upon the heart ... 28
Chapter 6	Understanding the Law 34
Chapter 7	God's solution—a new creation 41
Chapter 8	Like Father like sons 48
Chapter 9	Church growth…the apostolic way 59
Chapter 10	Religion versus the gospel 68
Chapter 11	Living from the finished work of Christ 78
Chapter 12	Prosperity is Christ 87
Chapter 13	Grace—the way home to the Father 99
Chapter 14	The bride awakes 107
Chapter 15	A finished work, an ascended church 117

Dedication

To Christopher, Hannah, Peter and Jotham.

> "My dear children, you come from God and belong to God…for the Spirit in you is far stronger than anything in the world."[1]
>
> John 4:4

> "It's in Christ that we find out who we are and what we are living for. Long before we first heard of Christ and got our hopes up, he had his eye on us, had designs on us for glorious living, part of the overall purpose he is working out in everything and everyone."[2]
>
> Ephesians 1:11–12

---

[1] The Message.
[2] The Message.

Introduction

"And he said to him, 'Son, you are always with me, and all that I have is yours'."[3]

Luke 15:31

In all my attempts to express how God's grace impacts my life, I inevitably seem to end up back at this verse. For a number of years now, I have been drawn again and again to this scene that Jesus described—the scene of a loving father speaking into the hurt of an estranged and deeply disappointed son. I want to return to this place often, for it was here, at this verse, that I had an encounter with God's Spirit. Like Jacob at Bethel, I want to declare to the world, "How awesome is this place!" At this place I found "the house of God and the gate of heaven." I saw the heart of God for me—the heart of a loving Father—and in that hour, the lies that had estranged me from Him in my mind began to break, like the cords that bound Samson as he awoke. Early the next morning when Jacob awoke, we are told that he took the stone that had been his pillow and set it up as a pillar and poured oil on it (Genesis 28:10–18). He wanted the very rock that spoke of his rejection now to speak of his revelation, for he knew that, far from being rejected, he now carried

---

[3] Unless otherwise indicated, scripture quotations are taken from the Holy Bible, New King James Version.

an assurance of God's presence and provision with him always. In Christ, all men have been given such a rock.

When a man sets up a memorial stone, it is an admission of weakness; man's tendency to forget. But it also speaks of his conviction that his experience was not just for him alone, but was a marker for others too. So it is with this book. I write it so that I may not forget His heart and so that others who happen upon it would inquire as to its meaning. When Jacob poured oil on his rock, it would have glistened in the light. Only the anointing of the Holy Spirit can transform a heart of stone into a beacon of light. Only by His grace can anyone know God, and here is the wonderful news of the gospel: through Jesus, grace and truth came and revealed the Father we never knew.

Phelim Doherty

Chapter 1

The unveiling of the church

"You were his enemies, separated from him by your evil thoughts and actions. Yet now he has reconciled you to himself through the death of Christ in his physical body. As a result, he has brought you into his own presence, and you are holy and blameless as you stand before him without a single fault. But you must continue to believe this truth and stand firmly in it. Don't drift away from the assurance you received when you heard the Good News."[4]

Colossians 1:21–23

For as long as most of us can remember, our desire as Christians has been for the church in our generation to experience the same explosive growth that the first-century church knew. In the search for a reason why we have not seen what we have long desired, we appear to return constantly to the conclusion that it must be because we are woefully inferior in our purity of life and devotion to God. This conclusion has led to one message being constantly presented as the solution to all of our problems. This message is preached in churches every week, the length and breadth of the nations. It comes

---

[4] New Living Translation.

in a thousand different forms, with ten thousand different titles and illustrations, and a multitude of scripture verses are called upon to justify it. What is this great message that the church is pinning her hopes upon? It can be summed up in just two words: try harder!

It comes as a surprise, then, to discover that the early church wasn't as different from us as we think. In its early years, the church was in the main made up of Jews, not Gentiles. They were a New Covenant people, brought up on stories of Old Covenant heroes. They, too, in their thinking, were a mixture of the Old and New Covenants, of Law and grace. They were as mixed up as we are today!

These Jewish Christians carried over into their new life the old-time religion which brought a deep reverence for Moses and the Law. Many Christians today call that mixture of Law and grace "balance." The apostle Paul had another name for the belief that the old wineskin can hold the new wine. He simply called it a perversion of the gospel (Galatians 1:6–7) and immediately recognized that this "balanced" message was undermining the pure foundation of Christ alone which he had laid in his churches. He saw the seductive appeal of the "try harder to be holier for God" message and repeatedly warned believers not to "drift away" from the gospel of God's grace that he had preached to them (Galatians 5:1–9). He recognized how the idea that we can move God by our piety (Romans 10:1–4) appealed to the pride of man. He saw it begin to infect the body of Christ and the inevitable resulting division, and in his letter to the Galatians he attacked the "try harder" message with the same zeal as a surgeon taking a knife to a cancer growing on the body. His scalpel was the gospel of grace and with it he set out to unbind a people who were alive, yet wrapped up so tightly in their own performance that they were blind to the fullness of what had been gifted to them; a totally new life, dead to sin, dead to the Law, and alive to God (Galatians 2:19, Romans 7:4). They were very much like Lazarus; risen from the dead but not aware of his new life because he was still bound by grave clothes. Lazarus, though bound and blinded, was not half dead or half alive. He was fully alive. He was just wearing the wrong clothes for a living man! Jesus's instruction was, "Loose him and let him go!" (John 11:44) For those who loved him, the first part of Lazarus they would surely have unveiled would have been his eyes.

That is a report of what is happening across the body of Christ, in every place where the Holy Spirit is opening the eyes of Christians to reckon themselves dead to sin and alive to God in Christ (Romans 6:3–11). The veil is being taken away; the veil of guilt and condemnation that covers the hearts and minds of believers who have not seen themselves as righteous in Christ, but still as sinners under the Law (2 Corinthians 3:9, 2 Peter 1:9). That veil has been a hindrance to believers boldly drawing near to their Father, in full assurance of His love for them and for the world (Hebrews 10:19–22). The result has been a church full of elder brothers who have sought to impress their distant father by the strength of their devotion to him. When sons live for so long like slaves, the danger is that they will end up resisting the message of their father's generosity, for it appears to take no account of their sacrifices (Luke 15:29–30, Romans 10:1–4).

The angel did not ask Mary to produce Christ, but to bear Christ (Luke 1:31). Not understanding the difference between producing and bearing will condemn you to a life of misery, as you strive to produce holiness through church life, rather than bear holiness through Christ life. The gospel of grace is the revelation of that difference.

The basis for receiving and experiencing the wholeness of life in Christ is Jesus's life. The work of the Holy Spirit is to unveil this life in every believer, and the effect of this unveiling is transformational (2 Corinthians 3:18).

No matter how many years we claim to have known Christ, let us never forget that the revelation of God we each carry is a gift (Ephesians 2:8–9). Our life in Christ is not, and never will be, a life achieved, but a life received by His grace. We must never resist the desire of the Father to show Himself to be more generous than our natural minds or experience have understood up to now (Ephesians 3:17–21). We must allow ourselves to be like little children in this matter if we want to live in the abundance of the life that the Father gives us and desires us to walk in (Matthew 18:3). It takes the gift of repentance (Acts 11:18) for man to humble himself, abandon all hope in his own strength, and daily continue to allow the Holy Spirit to reveal to him the greatest and most profound mystery that, in Christ, we stand before God holy and blameless, without a single fault (Colossians 1:21–23), and all by the grace of God. Let us allow Him to root us and ground us (Ephesians 3:17, Colossians 2:7) so deeply in this truth of our union with Him (1 Corinthians 6:17) that we, His body, grow up into His mind and see what He sees—the enormity of what has been freely given (1 Corinthians 2:12). Then, as mature sons, we will no longer hesitate to count our earthly achievements and institutions as nothing and enter joyfully into the simplicity of a Father's love for His children; a love that demands nothing and supplies everything (Romans 5:8, 8:32).

This gospel of God's grace announces nothing less than the abolition of religion. It is the most radical, revolutionary message in the world, for by leaving no place for pride, it is the only message that sets man free from himself. This makes it highly unpalatable to any person determined to justify himself through his performance. Hence, in each generation, men have found ways to water it down and turn a message about God's love for us into one about our love for Him (1 John 4:10).

We have taken a supernatural message and turned it into a mere natural one. The result is a spiritually immature church that sees strength primarily in natural terms, and church growth as being about congregation sizes and resources rather than revelation (Matthew 16:18). When the glitter of religious performance—what we can achieve for God—is peddled in the church as real gold for long enough, then we raise a generation of believers who know how to do things for God, but not how to be the children of a joyful Father! We raise a nation of holy orphans, who, not knowing their Father's righteousness as their spiritual DNA, live constantly trying to prove their parentage through their performance. The result is a church so sin-conscious and self-conscious that she is like a bride so insecure in her identity that she has buried the likeness of her Father beneath layers of makeup. Now when the world looks at the church, rather than seeing the likeness of Christ, it sees her insecurities, doubts, and fears written on her face and, assuming this is the likeness of her Father, they reject Him. It is extraordinary that even when so many in the church have settled for a Father who controls His children through the threat of punishment, so many in the world are holding out for a better Father! It comes at great cost to the church when we mix our behavior—what we need to do for God—with the pure gospel message that is entirely about what God has done for us. We have produced a Galatian church, a church estranged from the power of God (Galatians 5:4–6) that has forgotten that God's grace is not given to help us prune back sin in our lives to a respectable level, but has implanted in us an entirely new root, an entirely new tree, and an entirely new life (Galatians 2:20) that can no more be overcome by sin than light could be overcome by darkness.

God has such confidence in the power of His life, His grace, and His Spirit in us to overcome the power of sin that He has freed us entirely from the schoolmaster of the Law (Galatians 3:24–26). No longer is His blessing for man determined by man's performance, but simply by man's position in Christ. But God does not force His life on any man (1 Corinthians 13:4–7). The ability to receive God's generous gift of faith is given to men through the gospel message (Romans 10:17). The minds of so many have rejected religion because their hearts were made and are hungry for a Father, not a manager. They were made for sonship, not slavery (Romans 8:15). They were made for a Father who withholds no good thing from them and if they could only meet with Him as He really is and experience His embrace around them and His generosity to them, then they could enter into communion with Him, as the son of His love (Luke 15:20). It is through the proclamation of the undiluted gospel of God's grace that such meetings take place.

A church that shrinks back from preaching God's grace as unconditional does so because it knows nothing stronger than the threat of punishment to check men's behavior. What a tragic admission. If we really fear that lifting all threat of punishment off believers would cause them to run wild with sin, then what we are admitting is that years of ministry of our "gospel" have not changed the hearts of our hearers! They "behave" well, as children might behave under the supervision of a teacher, but in never being allowed out from under that yoke and its threats of punishment, they have been denied maturity. Their hearts have not been granted the opportunity to gain confidence in the power of the Spirit within them, to discover that God's grace toward them is not just the forgiveness of their sins, but the power to change the very root of their being and the very desires of their heart (Ezekiel 36:26, Titus 2:11–12).

This is because we were designed to live from the inside out, not from the outside in. For godliness to be authentic, we must be living the life we *want* to live, not merely the life we feel we *ought* to live. The heart was not built for trying, but for trusting and believing. Each of our lives is formed and transformed not by what we do, but by what our hearts have believed (Proverbs 4:23). We were formed as new creations when our hearts heard and believed in Christ and what He has done for us (2 Corinthians 5:17). The expression in our lives of that new form grows in the same way; by hearing about what Christ has done for us (Romans 10:17). We are transformed from glory to glory and we grow up into Christ as our hope remains anchored in His life in us, not in our life for Him (2 Corinthians 3:18). The gospel of grace fixes our gaze on Christ, for it reveals Him not just to be the author, but also the finisher, of our faith (Philippians 1:6, Hebrews 12:2).

Yet, having been supernaturally birthed and formed by the nourishment of the gospel, multitudes of believers enter a church system that subtly withdraws from them the pure food that brought life ("you only need to *believe* to become") and tries to grow believers on a far inferior message ("you need to *do* to become"). The gospel of God's grace is widely seen as a message to the world, but not to the church. Having been told that Christ has done enough to save us, once they enter the church many discover that, apparently, He hasn't done enough, for they are presented each week with a list of things they must do to finish what He started. The list varies from church to church, but the top ten dos and don'ts will usually include an immediately expected certain standard of behavior, level of financial giving, and correct language or "confession."

The work of the Holy Spirit is to bring such a revelation of sonship to each believer that fear is expelled and the fruit of Christ's life begins to thrive in the rich soil of a heart at rest. But this development is short-circuited and hindered by churches so eager to "grow" that they present performance rather than revelation as the way Christ promised He would build His church (Matthew 16:15–18). Young believers, thankful for what Christ has done, are only too eager to "do" something for Him and, full of hope, step onto the treadmill of "doing to become." This is the direction the prodigal son would have gone if the father had not point blank refused to allow him to be anything other than his son (Luke 15:20–24). Once we start down the road of trying to earn from God what He has already freely given to us (everything in Christ!), then our hearts are starved of the very rest they were made for. We were designed to be, not to do; to "be" still and know that He is God (Psalm 46:10). The extent to which the church has fallen from "being" to "doing" can be seen in cities around the world, where local churches actually exist in competition with each other rather than in union, for when we let men place our performance between us and God, we let them place it between us and our brethren also.

Only the revelation of the finished nature of salvation deprives the spirit of division of the soil of insecurity in which it roots and grows (1 Corinthians 3:21–23). Our hearts were designed to believe in the goodness of God, for it is only through believing in His good vision of us that we can be all that He sees us to be. Only the revelation of the Father we never knew causes us to be the children we never thought we were. He has kept His promise. He has not left us as orphans, for His Spirit cries out in us, "Abba Father," and that cry is awakening a generation to rise out of doing and into being, into being the body of Christ.

Chapter 2

Beginning in rest

"Come to Me, all you who labor and are heavy laden, and I will give you rest."

Matthew 11:28

We are used to thinking of rest as something that comes after we have completed what we need to do for the day. We talk about a well-earned rest and think about it as something to work toward. But the Christian life begins in rest; not a rest achieved, but a rest received.

To receive the life of Christ is to receive the life of one who has ceased his works and entered into His rest (Hebrews 4:10). To do this, we must cease trying to do what God has already done for us. We must stop trying to save ourselves. The Bible says that this will take some diligence on our part to stop striving, enter into God's rest, and remain there. In fact, we are told it may require us to make every effort to achieve this (Hebrews 4:11). When I think of the average churchgoer trying to enter into God's rest, the image of a salmon swimming upstream comes to mind, because the world and many church members are flowing in the opposite direction. The spirit of the world teaches us that we are what we do, so get busy doing if you want to be somebody. But the Spirit who comes from God reveals the enormity of how much has been freely given to us (1 Corinthians 2:12). The effect of this revelation; that the work of salvation was finished on the cross, brings a rest so profound to the human soul that we find ourselves being transformed into the image of God at rest (2 Corinthians 3:18).

The revelation of the relationship of a child and a loving father is one that brings rest to every fearful soul and restoration to a right relationship with God. The apostle Paul described this revelation as the very "power of God to save us" and named it "the righteousness of God" (Romans 1:16–17). The revelation that empowers us to live the Christ life is that the righteousness—the right life—we have been seeking to live for God is not something we have to attain through our performance (Romans 1:17). There is no required level of prayer to reach, or right confession to speak, or resources to give, before God will reward our efforts by blessing us (Ephesians 1:3). The reason is that one man took our place and prayed and confessed and gave all that had to be given, even His own life (Romans 5:19), so that we might stand today complete in Him (Colossians 2:10), and holy and blameless in God's sight (Ephesians 1:4).

God's own Holy Spirit confirms this good news (gospel) by filling our lives with His contentment and joy over us (Romans 5:5). The revelation of this truth that righteousness—the blessed life of God—is not a state to work toward (self-righteousness), but a gift to be freely received (the righteousness of God), is the key to experiencing the very power of God in salvation (Romans 1:16–17). The result of being persuaded of this truth is the restoration of rest and joy to the soul. St. Augustine famously pointed out that in being made for God, our souls would not find rest until they found Him. The news that Jesus, who knew no sin, was made sin for us so that we might be made the righteousness of God in Him (2 Corinthians 5:21) sounds almost too good to be true. We do not become righteous progressively, rather we were *made* righteous when we accepted

Christ's righteous life as our own. We cannot even boast of having the faith to believe, as even that faith is "not of ourselves but is the gift of God, not of works lest any man should boast"[5] (Ephesians 2:8–9). In other words, our complete salvation (justification and sanctification) is by Christ's work from first to last (Hebrews 12:2). The apostle Paul shared with the church in Galatia that the more we try to add what we do onto what Christ has done (the more religious we become!), the more we estrange ourselves from the very power of God. This is the great truth that the Holy Spirit reveals to every generation of believers. Any addition of Old Covenant-based requirements to the gospel effectively strips the message of its power (1 Corinthians 5:6, Galatians 5:9). The New Testament is full of warnings of the danger of adding anything to the simple message of the cross. "But I fear, lest somehow, as the serpent deceived Eve by his craftiness, so your minds may be corrupted from the simplicity that is in Christ" (2 Corinthians 11:3).

In response to this we could be forgiven for asking, "Then what exactly do we have to do if God has done it all for us?" To this question Jesus replied, "The work of God is this: to believe in the one He has sent"[6] (John 6:29). At first this appears too simple; too easy. But if it is so easy, how did we manage to mess it up and end up with thousands of different groupings and denominations, each claiming to have the truth? The answer brings us back to Paul's letter to the Galatians, for truly when it comes to making mistakes, there are no new ones! How did they, and we, manage to get entangled again in religion, when it was for freedom from slavery and performance that Christ set us free? (Galatians 5:1)

The problem is our pride. The gospel of grace leaves no room for boasting and if we do not let the truth that grace is unmerited, and that the Father *is* that generous, reign fully in our hearts, then we

---

[5] King James Version.
[6] New International Version.

will always seek to add our two cents, just to be sure. But with each tempting performance target we pride ourselves in seeking to reach, we further estrange ourselves, both from the power of His grace and from those to whom we have now started to compare ourselves (Galatians 5:4, James 4:6).

I believe the story that most beautifully communicates our struggle to receive grace, the life God offers us, and how we have succumbed instead to the temptation to make a life for ourselves, is Jesus's account of the parable of the prodigal son in Luke 15. He describes two sons, both hungering to be someone, to find the good life, and to seek the answer to their restless hearts through what they could achieve. The younger son leaves home, after demanding that his father give him the inheritance he should only receive upon his father's death. In effect, he is saying, "I want to live as if you are dead. I want to make a life for myself." He proceeds to do all the things that he thinks will bring him the good life he seeks, but is left empty and alone. From a Christian perspective, he does all the wrong things. The big shock of the story, however, is that the elder son, the one who sought to find the good life by staying at home and doing all the right things, also ends up empty, alone, and very angry.

Despite what you may have heard all your life, doing all the right things is not the way into the righteous life. Such a message only leaves people empty and angry, because their faith has actually been in themselves and in what they are doing for God, instead of in what He has done for them. At the end of the story, the father pleads with his elder son to put an end to his attempts to earn what the father has freely given. This is the same beautiful truth that the Holy Spirit is communicating to the church in this hour; "Son, you are always with me, and all that I have is yours" (Luke 15:31). Through his words and actions toward both sons, the father in Jesus's story is revealed to be abundantly loving and generous. This very truth was at the heart of Jesus's mission and ministry; to reveal to us the Father we never knew (John 14:9, 17:20–23).

Did it never strike you as a strange story for Jesus to tell? How can sons, who are loved so much, not know of the love of their own father? Yet is this not the story of our own nations and our own lives? Because of the lack of revelation of the generosity of the Father, many have turned their backs on the church and looked to the world for approval and acceptance. Others have kept going to church and toiled for years in the field of religion, appearing outwardly closer to the Father, but inwardly remaining frustrated, angry, and quick to pass judgment on those not working as hard as them.

In another parable, Jesus recounts the anger of workers toward the owner of a vineyard, who paid those who only worked for one hour the same wages as those who had worked all day (Matthew 20:1–16). Jesus describes their great offense at their master's generosity and the response of the vineyard owner, who declares "Am I not permitted to do what I choose with what is mine? [Or do you begrudge my being generous?] Is your eye evil because I am good?"[7] (Matthew 20:15).

Every generation takes the same offense to the scandalous generosity of the Father. Like the elder brother of the prodigal son, many of us have been trying so hard to impress our Father that we cannot see that it is we who have estranged ourselves from His grace (Galatians 5:4). The shocking truth of the gospel is that it is not God who distances himself from the church because He is offended by its sin, but it is the church who has consistently drawn back from the full power of the gospel because it is offended at God's generosity! By drawing back from His generosity we have drawn back from His rest.

---

[7] Amplified Bible. Classic Edition.

Chapter 3

The Father we never knew

> "When they heard these things they became silent; and they glorified God, saying, 'Then God has also granted to the Gentiles repentance to life'."
>
> Acts 11:18

If we see Jesus for who He really is we behold the glory of God, for He truly is the greatest revelation of the character of God (John 14:9). He is the "radiance of God's glory and the exact representation of His being"[8] (Hebrews 1:3). In 2 Corinthians 3:18 it is declared that simply beholding the glory of the Lord is enough to transform us into the same image we are looking at. In other words when a person begins to see God as He really is—how good He is, how generous He is, how loving He is—they cannot remain the same! That revelation brings a liberty from fear, and a freedom that changes their lives (John 8:32). The truth about the goodness and glory of God is powerful enough to bring about a transformation of the person from the inside out (a heart change). As the person's mind is overwhelmed with the truth about how good God is, their heart, their belief system, and the root of their own character are transformed. The Bible calls this a *metanoia* (Matthew 4:17) which

---

[8] New International Version.

leads to a metamorphosis (Romans 12:2). The fruit of this change of heart (*metanoia*) is seen in the actions of the person, because a heart at rest in the generosity of a loving Father produces a life of giving rather than grasping, or a life of love rather than sinning. Notice that it is the change of actions that follows the change of heart, not the other way around, and what produces a change of heart is revelation of truth. In other words, true repentance is both birthed and grows from the revelation of the true loving nature of God (Romans 2:4). Instead of *metanoia*, we use the word "repentance," but unfortunately the common understanding of repentance in the church moves the emphasis away from revelation (God's work in the heart) and toward renunciation (man's response in the flesh).

This is the power of the gospel of grace—the revelation of the true heart of God produces a true *metanoia*. Our hard hearts are melted, just as the prophet Ezekiel said they would be (Ezekiel 11:19, 36:26). Repentance that glorifies God is not something that men can be exhorted to, apart from the empowering influence of God's Spirit. No one achieves repentance without the grace of God. That is why the early church, on hearing about the conversion of Cornelius and his household, concluded not that the Gentiles had *achieved* repentance, but rather that God had "to the Gentiles granted repentance unto life"[9] (Acts 11:18). This gift was presented to them through the gospel.

How can we demand or expect people to repent if we withhold from them the means to do so? How can we demand them to repent if we have not declared to them the gospel—the very message concerning the grace of God—that is in itself the power that changes a person's belief system, for the heart of man has never heard such glad tidings of good things (Romans 10:13–15). Truly until Jesus came, no man's mind had ever imagined how generous and good our Father in

---

[9] King James Version.

heaven really is (John 1:18, 1 Corinthians 2:9). True repentance can only be granted through a revelation of Christ, for it is more than just turning from sin; it is turning to God (Acts 20:21).

The Father that Jesus revealed was so much more abundantly gracious and generous than any man had ever seen, that John openly declares in his Gospel that until Jesus came, it was as if no man, no prophet, and no patriarch had ever seen God.

> "No man has ever seen God at any time; the only unique Son, or the only begotten God, who is in the bosom [in the intimate presence] of the Father, He has declared Him [He has revealed Him and brought Him out where He can be seen; He has interpreted Him and He has made Him known]."[10]
> (John 1:18)

Jesus knew that the religious establishment would become His greatest opponent and everywhere He and, later, His disciples taught, that proved true (Matthew 21:45–46). Teachings such as the story of the prodigal son, which reveals a father so generous that He gives Himself away entirely, not just to the deserving but to the undeserving, and makes no difference between them, scandalized the religious establishment. They understood that the revelation Jesus brought of the generous Father was effectively abolishing religion, for, unlike religion, the gospel isn't a message about how much we need to love God, but of how much God loves us (1 John 4:10). Religion is all about what you need to do for God. The gospel is all about what God has done for you.

Jesus came declaring that salvation wasn't about us trying to reach God by what we could do for Him; it is about God reaching us by what He would do for us. Jesus was the substance and reality of His

---

[10] Amplified Bible. Classic Version.

The Father we never knew

own message. That's why the most common verse in the Bible used to sum up the gospel is John 3:16, "For God so loved the world that he gave his one and only Son, that whoever believes in him shall not perish but have eternal life."[11] This declares the good news is that all God is asking man to do is to believe in what He has done. In effect, what we have to do is receive the gift of His son. We get what we didn't earn or deserve. That's called grace.

This good news about the amazing grace of God was never meant to be mixed with religion, because religion is the antithesis of the gospel (Romans 11:6). That's why Jesus, and, later, the apostles, were opposed everywhere, continually and most strongly by the group that had most to lose from a message that God has done it all for you: the religious.

The gospel declares that our Father in heaven has held nothing back from us, and that He loves us so much that He couldn't wait around for us to deserve His love because we would never be able to attain it (John 3:16). Our Father in heaven has—like Jesus's description of the father in Luke 15—run to meet us, stretched open His arms, wrapped them around us in our unrighteousness, and dressed us with His very own best robe. Now you might say, "Did I miss something? When did God ever put His arms out for me?" He stretched them out on a cross outside Jerusalem two thousand years ago. There He embraced all the sin, sickness, and pain of the world Himself (Galatians 3:13). He did that so that whoever recognized that Jesus did that for them—that Jesus died for their sins—could believe in Him and receive the Father's embrace, His life, His Spirit, and all that comes with sonship (John 3:14–15).

To receive Jesus is to receive the robe, the ring, and the shoes from the Father; His righteousness, His name, and His fatherhood (sons

---

[11] New International Version.

wore shoes, while servants tended to be barefoot). As the apostle John said, "Yet to all who did receive him, to those who believed in his name, he gave the right to become children of God"[12] (John 1:12). The gift of a life with God is freely given. The only thing required of us is to accept the gift.

That sounds too simple for most of us who have been trying to earn God's love and blessing for years. That's why the elder brother objected to how the father had given his blessing to the younger brother. He was in effect saying, "It can't be as simple as that. I have been preparing myself through hard work for years to be fit to receive your blessing and then my brother gets it, simply by asking for it!" The elder brother in us too, on hearing the gospel of grace, thinks, "This sounds too simple. There has to be more to it than simply to ask. Even a child could do that!" But listen again to Jesus's words to His disciples: "Truly I tell you, anyone who will not receive the kingdom of God like a little child will never enter it"[13] (Mark 10:15). The pride of man always wants to mix something of his own efforts into the free gift of salvation, but to mix a little self-effort in with the gospel "leavens the whole lump" (Galatians 5:9). "You ran well. Who hindered you from obeying the truth? This persuasion does not come from Him who calls you. A little leaven leavens the whole lump" (Galatians 5:7–9).

Scripture exhorts us to stand firm in the liberty of the gospel of grace and not to be ensnared again by any mixed message of grace and works, for such thinking will estrange us from Christ and the power of His Spirit (Galatians 5:1–4, 3:2). Salvation comes entirely from the life of Christ (Hebrews 12:2). You are saved by His sinless, perfect life in you (Colossians 3:4). It is from His life in you, and His life alone, that the fruit of the Holy Spirit comes (Galatians 5:22–23). We can't grow figs from the root of a thorn bush, no matter

---

[12] New International Version.
[13] New International Version.

The Father we never knew

how much we prune the tree! Religion can only produce behavior modification, but not the inner transformation and birthing of an entirely new life that the Spirit of God produces (John 3:6). We are to remain in the faith, the life that the gospel of grace imparts to us. Without Him we can produce nothing (John 15:5). He is the seed and the source of eternal life. We need only let His Word and His love take root in our hearts and produce salvation (Ephesians 3:16–19).

The angel did not ask Mary to produce Christ, but to bear Christ (Luke 1:31). His seed in us is powerful enough to grow the fruit of His life and it is an overcoming life (Gal.5:22, Gal.4:19, John 16:33) No matter how plagued our lives are with sins, the power of His grace and His life in us is like light in the darkness. The darkness never overcomes the light.

When people asked Jesus what works God required them to do, His answer was recorded in John 6:28–29; "Then they asked him, "What must we do to do the works God requires?" Jesus answered, "The work of God is this: to believe in the one he has sent."[14] Religion is complicated because it is all about what you need to do for God and the list of requirements seems endless. The gospel is very simple, because it is about what God has done for you and it can be summed up in four words: "Jesus Christ and Him crucified"[15] (1 Corinthians 2:2).

In a very real sense, Christ and His crucifixion abolished religion. Religion is all about the distance between you and God and how you can narrow the gap. Each religion has its own list of requirements: stop doing that, do this, eat that, go there…and on and on it goes. Religion holds out the promise of getting closer to God. A better day or a new experience is always coming soon, but never seems to

---

[14] New International Version.
[15] King James Version.

arrive. Religion flourishes in Christian churches through teaching that infers that believers remain cut off from God by their sins; that He is holy, but they are still unholy. That barrier between a holy God and an unholy people was represented in the temple in Jerusalem by a large curtain that separated the holy of holies—where the presence of God resided—and the rest of the temple. The moment Jesus died on the cross, that curtain was torn from top to bottom (Matthew 27:51). No one understood at the time what that meant and it took the outpouring and the leading of the Holy Spirit for the early church to understand gradually that religion as they understood it—man trying to get holy enough for God—had been abolished (Acts 10:28).

It took time for the early Christians to alter their way of thinking to this new reality, because they had been brought up under the Old Covenant, and related to God in a performance-based way. Under the Old Covenant, the blessing of God was determined by a person's performance. Be obedient to God's commands and you will be blessed (Deuteronomy 28:1–14), but be disobedient and you will be cursed (Deuteronomy 28:15–68). The Bible describes this mind-set as a veil over their understanding. For them to fully see the Father as He really was, this veil had to be removed (2 Corinthians 3:14–16).

In many ways, the Jewish early church, steeped in Old Covenant traditions and thinking, was alive in Christ but still wrapped up in the dead clothes of the Law. They were very much like Lazarus; risen from the dead but not aware of his new life because he was still bound by grave clothes. Look again at how what happened next is described in John 11:44: "And he who had died came out bound hand and foot with graveclothes, and his face was wrapped with a cloth. Jesus said to them, 'Loose him, and let him go'."

This is the ministry of the Holy Spirit across the body of Christ, equipping ascension ministries to loose believers from their preoccupation with self, through reckoning themselves dead to sin and alive to God in Christ (Romans 6:3–11). Eyes are opened to our victory in Christ as the gospel of grace pulls back the veil of guilt and condemnation that lies over the hearts and minds of believers who have not seen themselves as righteous in Christ for years, but still as sinners under the Law (2 Peter 1:9). The sin-conscious, self-conscious believer struggles to boldly draw near to his Father, in full assurance of His love for him and for the world. Instead, like the elder brother in Luke 15, we work hard out in the field of religion, seeking to impress a distant Father by the strength of our devotion to Him. The longer this continues, the more vulnerable we become to our hope moving from what God has done for me, to what I have done for God. Now, like the elder son, our approach to the Father follows the pattern of Cain rather than Abel (Genesis 4:4–5). This attitude can sometimes be heard in the prayers of believers when a respected Christian leader falls ill. We are quick to remind God of their years of faithful service, when in fact there has only ever been one life of faithful service that man can appeal to as the basis for receiving and experiencing the wholeness of life in Christ: Jesus's life. The work of the Holy Spirit is to unveil this life to every believer, for the effect of this unveiling is transformational (2 Corinthians 3:18).

Chapter 4

The apostolic foundation

> "According to the grace of God which was given to me, as a wise master builder I have laid the foundation, and another builds on it. But let each one take heed how he builds on it. For no other foundation can anyone lay than that which is laid, which is Jesus Christ."
>
> 1 Corinthians 3:10–11

We must preach a message that roots and grounds people in the love of God for them, not expect them to build a life on the shaky foundation of their love for God (1 John 4:10). Faulty foundations lead to cracks and divisions in a building. The foundation for every life and every work that carries the name "Christian" must be Christ alone. I believe this is why one of the ascension ministry gifts that Christ has placed in His church is that of the apostle. Apostles are the guardians of the foundations laid in each generation of believers and their calling is to ensure that no other foundation is laid except Christ Jesus (1 Corinthians 3:9–11). Spirit gives birth to spirit. The life of a Christian is nothing less than the life of Christ, and the life of Christ in every generation is nothing less than supernatural. The Christ life still saves, heals and delivers when lived by the faith of the Son of God in us (Galatians 2:20). That faith is quickened in us by hearing the truth that God has withheld nothing of His life from us (Romans 10:17).

But how can we believe this message and grow in the Christ life if, instead of hearing about what God has *already* freely given us, we are reared on a diet of messages that speak of what He *would* give us—such as healing, provision, and blessing—if only we would try and be a bit more holy! Such messages sound great, but they are in fact a product of the spirit of the world, not the Spirit of God. The Spirit of God comes to reveal to us what has been freely given to us, not what we can earn (1 Corinthians 2:12). The tragic irony that Paul lamented to the Galatians was that the more a church gives its people the impression that separating themselves from sin will move the hand of God, the less they can see clearly how God's hand has already moved (Galatians 3:1). In other words, to elevate man to the position of saving himself from his sins is to replace Christ as the life that saves us. The scriptures have a name for this spirit of the world that replaces Christ's performance with man's. It is the spirit of the anti-Christ (1 John 2:18, 2:22, 4:3, 2 John 1:7).

By pointing us to our own performance, messages that infer that we can awaken God to action subtly wrap us up in ourselves again, until spiritually we resemble Lazarus; alive from the dead, but so wrapped up in the trappings of our old soulish life and our sense of lack that we wander blindly ineffective in our new life (2 Peter 1:9). In short, we live like the heir to a vast fortune, who, without the faith to see and grow into his true identity, remains too immature to live in the fullness of his inheritance. Instead he remains with the mind of a child, restricted to a list of dos and don'ts and the threat of punishment to keep him from harming himself.

Multitudes of Christians remain this way, and without a revelation of their new identity and position in Christ, they cling to their attempted obedience to God's commands, as a child in fear of the world clings to the hand of its schoolmaster. This was the very illustration that the apostle Paul declared to the Galatians, as he contrasted the restricted life of immature believers with the liberty that faith brings (Galatians 3:23–27). Two thousand years later, many Christians are still clinging to that schoolmaster of the Law, and the communities in which they live are the poorer for it.

Messages that do not minister the truth of who Christians already are in Christ leave them immature and vulnerable to deception (Ephesians 4:11–15). Religion uses the fear of punishment to try and force an outer change; mere behavior modification (if you will do this, then God will do that, but if you don't…). This type of message looks and sounds good to the carnal man, for his pride is attracted to the idea that he can influence God, but flesh can only ever give birth to flesh (John 3:6). If the "gospel" you are sitting under causes you to compare your performance with that of others, then it is not of the Holy Spirit, who comes to reveal to us a God who has already freely given all He has (Romans 8:32, 1 Corinthians 3:21–23, Ephesians 1:3). Such a message leaves no room for boasting, religious posturing, or pride (Ephesians 2:8–9). This is one of the most remarkable features of the gospel of grace; to the carnal man it sounds arrogant and boastful to declare yourself to be righteous, at peace with God, and to already have in Christ all that you need. But to receive this message for yourself will require coming to the end of yourself and breaking pride in your own ability (2 Corinthians 1:8–9).

Only the gospel of God's grace can liberate a soul from the religious deception of appearing to have your hope in God, when in truth it has been in yourself all along. The difference is felt in the joy you experience. Jesus promised that His yoke was easy and His burden light. If you are tired and worn out as a Christian and constantly find yourself comparing your devotion to Christ with others, then it is most likely because the message you have heard has directed your attention to yourself. Someone has mixed in a little leaven of the Law with the gospel and the result is no gospel at all (Galatians 1:6–7). The result is powerless Christianity, what we could call "churchianity," and many of us as believers have been bound up in it for years. To such a church, the Lord speaks by His Spirit, "Loose him and let him go."

This is why we should not be ashamed to preach this simple gospel of grace, for it is the power of God to loose the church into the fullness of the Christ life. This Christ life is completely transcultural, for it is not rooted in the basic traditions or cultures of this world, which appeal to the natural senses (the appearance of holiness through mere words or rituals). Whenever the church in any generation or culture begins to rely more on its traditions, rather than on the radical grace of the leading of the Holy Spirit, we find that barriers begin to rise between the church and the world. Believers now present a "mixed gospel" of grace and works that adds to the pure gospel of grace certain cultural or denominational conditions to membership of Christ's body. Within a generation or two, the inevitable result becomes a "church" that has effectively cut itself off from both the community it is seeking to reach and the very means to reach it; the radical grace of God. In refusing to minister the most relevant message in the world to any culture or generation—pure grace—the modern church in so many places has been left grasping for the latest church growth fad in increasingly desperate attempts to reach their generation. By trying so hard to impress the Father, the insecurity of the elder brother church causes it to start to see other groups of believers in a local area not as family, but as competition. When believers lose the revelation of their total acceptance in Christ, they grow so sin-conscious and self-conscious that they can actually become a stumbling block to that local population from coming to Christ. How it must grieve the Father's heart to know that not only do elder brothers estrange themselves from intimacy with Him, but standing out there in all their hurt and piety, they put off so many others whom the Father has invited to share in the joy of His salvation (Luke 15:28). If the prodigal son had met his elder brother before his father, would he have made it home?

But who can break this cycle of decline, where a church has got so wrapped up in its own identity and history that it can no longer see its true identity and foundation for all the denominational wood, hay and rubble obscuring it? Which ministry in the church carries this particular grace? I will let an apostle give the answer: "According to the grace of God which is given unto me as a wise masterbuilder, I have laid the foundation and another builds on it. But let every man take heed how he builds on it. For no other foundation can any man lay than that is laid, which is Jesus Christ" (1 Corinthians 3:10–11). Much of Paul's ministry as an apostle was not just to establish Christ as the foundation of every believer's life (Colossians 2:6–10), but to go back and clear away from that foundation any cultural or religious baggage that was being introduced by churches as an addition to the pure gospel of God's grace (Galatians 3:1–3).

The proliferation of competing groups in the church, the stagnation into works, and the dearth of the dynamic of the Spirit can largely be traced to the dilution of the power of the gospel. This has happened through the countless small additions that men have added, each subtly moving the foundation of our hope off Christ's performance and back onto ours. I believe that Christ's gift to His church of apostles was to guard against this danger, for He knew in each generation there would be a great need of fathers. The difference in the church between fathers and managers is that fathers are not goal driven. To have the father's heart for the church is to see her as already pleasing to God and such vision leads her into resting on Christ's work. A manager's focus on results can subtly instill the belief that the church would be more pleasing to the Father if she achieved more, and such vision drives her into restlessness and a sense of never being good enough. To this day, Marthas in the church remain confounded that Marys refuse to join their church clean-up programs, and Marys remain astonished that Marthas are so busy for Christ, but hardly know Him!

This heart of the Father—His ability to see Himself in his children and, through his affirming words, establish them in their identity as His cherished offspring—roots and grounds believers in a foundation that is strong enough to resist the winds of performance-based identity that blow through the world and the church.

Chapter 5

Grace—His divine influence upon the heart

> "But by the grace of God I am what I am, and His grace toward me was not in vain; but I labored more abundantly than they all, yet not I, but the grace of God which was with me."
>
> 1 Corinthians 15:10

The only truth powerful enough to change a human heart from "grasper" to "giver" is the gospel of Jesus Christ; the good news of the grace of God. Paul declared the gospel as "the power of God unto salvation"[16] (Romans 1:16). If the "gospel" we are preaching is not bringing about a heart change in those receiving it, then we are not communicating the same gospel (Galatians 1:6).

The gospel is the truth about the love of God for man revealed in Jesus Christ, and it has the power to radically change the way we think about God, ourselves, and the world around us. John the Baptist (Matthew 3:1–2) and Jesus (Matthew 4:17) both described this change in thinking in one word: *metanoia*. Unfortunately the

---

[16] King James Version.

poor translation of this Greek word into English as "repent" has led to a diminished understanding of what true *metanoia* means. Our popular understanding of the words "repent" and "repentance" is that they refer to feeling sorrow or contrition for one's actions, with this sorrow leading to a change of lifestyle. There is nothing wrong in itself with feeling remorse for sin and a desire to change, but this alone does not define true *metanoia*. This is because someone can feel guilt and remorse over sin and attempt to change their actions, without any revelation of the true character of God; the revelation of Christ. Unfortunately this attempt to change ourselves by being "sorry enough" has led many into a hopeless cycle of repenting again and again but never finding victory over ever-present sin. The problem with this definition of *metanoia* is that it focuses on a change of action, but the truth is that our actions are only the fruit. The root is our belief system—what we believe about God and ourselves. Jesus's ministry and teaching brought about a change of belief or heart, from which a change in actions would flow. Jesus dealt with the root of man's problem, not just the branches. Pruning a thorn bush back closely enough will never turn it into a fig tree!

Everywhere Jesus went, He confronted the Pharisees and teachers of the Law who were trying to get people to "repent" of their ways using the Law (by saying "thou shalt not"). The Law has no power to change people because that was not its function. It simply reveals a person's sin and his inability to change on his own. It does this by setting out a goal of holiness that is impossible to attain naturally (Galatians 2:16). Without the power to change our heart motives internally, the religious leaders were simply demanding outward change and behavior modification. They had strong enough willpower to manage to keep the many rules and regulations, and gave the impression of "holiness," but Jesus was scathing of this act reminiscent of "cleaning the outside of the cup while leaving the inside dirty" (Luke 11:39). He pointed out that this type of "repentance" produced men who were like the white-washed tombs of the day; clean on the outside but full of corruption and death on the inside (Matthew 23:27).

Any similar "gospel" message that leaves you with the impression that you can change your life by your own willpower, or repent by trying harder to be good, without a radical change in your thinking, will ultimately leave you exhausted and burnt out.

Old-time religion and the belief that it is the sacrifices we make for God that gain us His presence and His blessing may make us feel good temporarily, but they cannot take away the veil of the consciousness of our own sin that prevent us from "drawing near with a true heart in full assurance of faith." (Hebrews 10:19–22).

That condemning feeling that no matter how hard you try, you still aren't good enough for communion with God, is a killer. It kills intimacy with God, which is why Paul declared to the Corinthians that "the letter kills"[17] (2 Corinthians 3:6). Under a Law mind-set, the Bible says that people live with this veil between them and God that they can't break through. This belief in their hearts that they are not good enough for God effectively acts as a barrier to them drawing near to Him and knowing intimacy with Him.

At the point in a wedding ceremony where the couple have just been married, the minister declares the following words of Jesus: "What therefore God has joined together, let no man separate."[18] At that moment, it is traditional for the groom to kiss his bride, but there can be no such intimacy without the bride's veil first being drawn back. When we recognize sin-consciousness in the believer as a barrier to intimacy with God (Hebrews 10:1–3, 22), we can see that, far from accusing the brethren and continually reminding them of their sin, the work of the Holy Spirit in the church is to lift up the

---

[17] New International Version.
[18] New American Standard Bible.

power of the cross and to unveil to believers that they have been made righteous in God's sight (Colossians 1:22). The Holy Spirit and the Father are not in disagreement. The Father has declared that our sins are as far removed from Him as the East is from the West (Psalm 103:12). The Holy Spirit is not out to undo the Father's work! Our natural minds struggle to accept this truth.

One of the fears we have is that we will abuse such freedom. We fear that, without the threat of God turning His back on us if we sin, we will not be able to restrain ourselves from indulging in sin (Romans 6:1). This is the argument that grace could be used as a license to sin. If we stop for a moment and ask ourselves why we are afraid of such grace, the sad answer is that we each have such a poor record of self-control that we don't trust ourselves to be free. We actually believe that where grace abounds, sin will abound much more, despite the fact that the promise of God is the exact opposite (Romans 5:20). Part of the reason for our deep suspicion that grace will not result in victory over sin, but will weaken our defenses, is the common misunderstanding of what the grace of God actually is.

Many believers see grace as merely the absence of a penalty for sin, akin to an eternal amnesty for crime. They see grace as the forgiveness of all of our sins. Great though that is, the grace of God extends much further than the forgiveness of our sins. The grace of God is not merely the absence of *something* hanging over our lives, it is the living presence of *someone* in our lives (Ephesians 3:17). With grace, not only are our sins forgiven, but we are made an entirely new creation, indwelt by a power much greater than sin (2 Corinthians 5:17). Being afraid that the grace of God will cause us to sin is like fearing that when the sun rises, the darkness will be able to resist it and remain! This is confirmed by Strong's definition of the Greek word *charis*, which we translate as "grace." His definition is, "Grace: The Divine influence upon the heart and its reflection in the life, including gratitude." (Strong's G5485)

This divine influence is the ministry of the Holy Spirit, whose revelation is like light to our souls (John 16:13). He reveals the things which have been freely given to us (1 Corinthians 2:12) and in the light of God's generosity, our attempts to merit His blessing through our own efforts are revealed to avail nothing. "Neither circumcision nor uncircumcision avails anything, but faith working through love" (Galatians 5:6).

To see what Christ has done in you is a life-changing experience. It is like seeing, as if in a mirror, that your primary identity is no longer rooted in the first Adam (sinner) but in the last Adam (Christ). As the Holy Spirit continues to persuade our hearts and open our eyes to behold the glorious truth that we are children of God and joint heirs with Christ (Romans 8:16, Ephesians 1:18, Colossians 1:27), we are being transformed into His image from glory to glory (2 Corinthians 3:18).

Think of this growth in the Christ life like a seed within us (Matthew 13:31–32, Luke 8:5, 1 Peter 1:23). An acorn contains everything that the mature oak tree is. When we received Christ, we received our new life complete (Colossians 2:10). Now what remains is for us to grow up into the fullness of this life (Galatians 4:19, Ephesians 4:15). Just as a garden blossoms the more it is exposed to the sun, so our souls will blossom with the fruit of the Spirit as we learn to remain in the Son (John 15:5). The Holy Spirit teaches us to rest our faith in the power of His imperishable seed within us (1 Peter 1:23), rather than in our gardening skills! He is the finisher as well as the author of our faith. He will complete the good work He has begun in us (Philippians 1:6). Our role is to allow Him to do so (Colossians 3:15–16). So let the peace and the life of God rule your heart. Let the Holy Spirit establish you, root you, and ground you in one soil only; the love of the Father (Ephesians 3:17), for it is only by the grace of God that you are found in Him.

Only true *metanoia* leads to true metamorphosis (Romans 12:2). Let the Holy Spirit pull back the veil. Reckon yourself dead to sin and alive to God in Christ Jesus (Romans 6:11). True *metanoia* is for you to believe what God believes about you! The gospel of grace is the mind of Christ. It is how He sees you—totally accepted, totally perfected, and holy and blameless before Him (Colossians 1:22). See as He sees and you shall live as he lives (Matthew 6:22). Let His love mature and perfect you, driving out your fear and filling you with His love, and you shall be as your Father in heaven is (Matthew 5:43–48, 1 John 4:8). Remain rooted in the truth of His true nature and His grace (John 1:14). Be diligent to enter into His rest over you (Hebrews 4:11). Stand firm in this truth of His love for you, rooted and established in it and growing in it.

Do not let the boasts of religion beguile you away from the simplicity that is in Christ (2 Corinthians 11:3). Beware messages and messengers whose focus is on how much more you should be doing for God. They look and sound zealous for God, but in holding up your sin before you, they are only tempting you back to trying to establish your own righteousness (Romans 10:1–4). That is to point you down a powerless cul-de-sac; an alluring dead end that much of the church has wandered down. You cannot walk that way and at the same time be living in the power of the righteousness that comes from God (Galatians 5:1–9). Lift your eyes higher than yourself and fix them on Christ (Hebrews 12:2). Humility is not a matter of thinking less of yourself, but rather thinking of yourself less. To live knowing how much you have been given as a Christian is to live a life that overcomes all the trouble this world can bring (John 16:33). The knowledge that the gospel of grace brings is the most powerful seed in the world and produces eternal fruit: the life of Christ.

Chapter 6

Understanding the Law

> "Therefore by the deeds of the law no flesh will be justified in His sight, for by the law is the knowledge of sin. But now the righteousness of God apart from the law is revealed, being witnessed by the Law and the Prophets, even the righteousness of God, through faith in Jesus Christ, to all and on all who believe."
>
> Romans 3:20–22

Regardless of our religious backgrounds, the one truth that applies to us all is that when God looks at us, He sees past the person we appear to be and sees who we really are (1 Samuel 16:7). The Bible often refers to this true identity as our "heart," and Jesus said that it is out of our hearts that all our words and actions flow (Luke 6:45). When we understand that the root of our behavior is the state of our hearts, then we can see that trying to change our behavior without a change of heart is like trying to chop down a tree by pruning the branches.

Unfortunately much religious practice in our nation, across all traditions, is based on the mistaken belief that God wants us to try harder to prune ourselves of sin. Divisions have abounded in our society as we have become experts in examining each other's branches. Many of us have grown up with the belief that God's Law and commandments are there to help us overcome sin. The truth, then, that God's Law was not given to help you overcome sin, but to help sin overcome you, comes as a bit of a shock! (Romans 3:19)

The Law was given to reveal two truths to us: what sin is, and our total incapacity to overcome it in our own strength (Romans 3:20). The Law is the mirror that reveals sin in us, much like an X-ray or a scan will reveal hidden disease. If it does its job properly, the Law should reveal to us that our sin condition is terminal and that no amount of religious behavior or self-effort will overcome our sin, rather, sin has completely overcome us. Listen to the apostle Paul explain to the Romans how God's commandments, rather than help us overcome sin, provide the opportunity for sin to strengthen its hold on us; "But sin, seizing the opportunity afforded by the commandment, produced in me every kind of coveting. For apart from the law, sin was dead. Once I was alive apart from the law; but when the commandment came, sin sprang to life and I died"[19] (Romans 7:8–9).

But why would God want us to see ourselves overcome by sin, incapable of making ourselves holy? Because as long as we think we can save ourselves, we will never see our need of a Savior. No one who thinks their heart will heal itself agrees to a heart transplant!

The commandments of God were given, not so that we could make ourselves holy, but to show us that we can't make ourselves holy and so to prepare us for the truth that God Himself is the only one who can! "By the Law is the knowledge of sin" (Romans 3:20). The Law was given to lead us to one conclusion: that we need a Savior.

---

[19] New International Version.

"Therefore the law was our tutor to bring us to Christ, that we might be justified by faith. But after faith has come, we are no longer under a tutor" (Galatians 3:24–25).

To those who recognized themselves as incapable of overcoming sin, Jesus preached grace; that through receiving Him as their Savior, God would freely give them the holy life that they could never attain through a lifetime of religious effort (Luke 15:18–24, John 1:17).

But to those who thought that their own religious observance of the Law was making them holy, Jesus preached the Law, to reveal to them that the standard of God's holiness was too high for them ever to attain. In Matthew 5:20–48, Jesus raises the bar of holiness required by God to an impossibly high level, not to exhort us to try harder, but to bring us to the end of all our religious posturing. This passage begins with Him declaring, "For I tell you that unless your righteousness surpasses that of the Pharisees and the teachers of the law, you will certainly not enter the kingdom of heaven."[20] In case anyone misses the point that the standard required is perfection, He finishes by saying, "Be perfect, therefore, as your heavenly Father is perfect."[21]

So the bad news is that the righteousness, or perfection, we need is nothing short of God's own righteousness. God only has one standard of good and that is Himself (Mark 10:18). Any religion that tells you that you can become a good person through doing good things does not have God's same standard of good. No amount of telling a thorn bush that it is an apple tree will ever make it produce apples! An apple tree is an apple tree because its root is an apple tree root. There is no way any man or woman can ever become "good" as God is good, unless they receive the very nature of God as their nature; unless He becomes their root. Jesus declared this truth when

---

[20] New International Version.
[21] New International Version.

He said "I am the vine, you are the branches. He who abides in Me, and I in him, bears much fruit; for without Me you can do nothing" (John 15:5).

This is a very important truth. Before we can receive the good news about what God has given us through Christ, we must give up on any false hope that we can become like God on our own. Satan's original lie to Eve was the same: that we can become like God by what we do (Genesis 3:4–5). No one agrees to accept a heart transplant unless they are first convinced that they will die without one. Are you convinced of your need? Are you convinced yet, that apart from God giving you His nature and His goodness, that you can never be good alone? If you are not, then you will remain trapped in religion, happy to keep trying to improve yourself, thinking that God is pleased with all your sacrifices. God is not pleased that you think you can become good like Him without the gift of His nature. As long as you seek to establish your own goodness, you are rejecting His gift of Christ, and how could God be pleased with anyone rejecting His Son? (Romans 10:1–4) As long as you try to be good through doing good things, that old life, independent from God, will be the only life you have, and if you die independent from Him, that is how you will remain forever (Mark 8:36).

The Law was not given so that you could become a good person through obeying it, but rather that you could begin to see that God's idea of good is beyond you and only found in Him (Galatians 3:24). The Law was a shadow of God's goodness, but Jesus was always the substance (Hebrews 10:1, Colossians 2:17). Don't look to your obedience of God's commands as your hope of salvation. Despite the impression many in church may have given you, your record at keeping God's commandments is not your hope of salvation. God does not save people by their imperfect obedience to His Law, but by Christ's perfect obedience (Romans 5:19). His record was exchanged for yours at the cross (2 Corinthians 5:21). Yes, read that again and keep reading it until you feel something very deep within your heart beginning to stir. That will be joy being born in you, the joy of knowing that you don't have to carry the burden of trying to save yourself anymore, for Jesus carried that for you (Matthew 11:28–30).

The good news of the gospel is that by accepting Jesus Christ as your Lord and Savior, God's own righteousness is freely gifted to you (Romans 5:17). This is beautifully summed up by the apostle Paul in his letter to the Ephesians. "For it is by grace you have been saved, through faith—and this is not from yourselves, it is the gift of God—not by works, so that no one can boast"[22] (Ephesians 2:8–9). There is still a need today for some to hear the impossibly high standards of the Law, for there are still groups of people who think that they can make themselves righteous through their own good behavior. We could call these the "self-righteous," and they are found both outside and inside the church. Those outside the church may seek to justify themselves by believing "I have never done anyone any harm." Those inside the church do so by believing "I can bring my purity to a level where God will bless me."

Both are making the same mistake for the same reason. They both believe that God blesses us on the basis of *our* lives, *our* obedience, and *our* holiness. What allows them to believe this is their assumption that God's standard of holiness is attainable. But God does not, and cannot, bless our best efforts to be right in our own strength, for as a loving Father, He wants us dressed in the best He can give us; the robe of His righteousness (Luke 15:22) and not "filthy rags," which is how He describes our righteousness compared to His (Isaiah 64:6).

God's holiness is gifted to us on the basis of just one person's obedience and life, and that is the life of Jesus Christ. That is the best news you will ever hear in this world. Every time you think your obedience or

---

[22] New International Version.

lack of it determines God's attitude to you, remember Romans 5:19: "For as by one man's disobedience many were made sinners, so also by one Man's obedience many will be made righteous."

Where do people get the idea that God blesses us on the basis of our performance, our lives, and our holiness? It comes from misunderstanding the purpose of the Law. Many people both outside and inside the church still use the Law to "try harder" to overcome the sin in their lives, because they think that is the purpose of the Law. But as we have seen from Romans 7:9, that is like using petrol to try and put out a fire!

Through our own willpower we are capable of keeping some of the Law, but considering that scripture declares that to keep only some of the Law is to break it all (James 2:10), then to attempt to deal with our sin through our willpower is like trying to empty the Atlantic ocean with a bucket (with a hole in it!). "Therefore by the deeds of the law no flesh will be justified in His sight, for by the law is the knowledge of sin. But now the righteousness of God apart from the law is revealed, being witnessed by the Law and the Prophets, even the righteousness of God, through faith in Jesus Christ, to all and on all who believe. For there is no difference; for all have sinned and fall short of the glory of God" (Romans 3:20–23).

Many Christians pay lip service to the truth of God's grace. They believe that they were justified (made right with God) by faith in Jesus's death on the cross, but they do not believe that Jesus's blood is a sufficient sacrifice to continue to deal with their sin forever (Hebrews 10:12). In other words, they believe that a certain level of sin in the life of a Christian will overcome the power of the blood of Jesus, and that a certain level of sin in their lives will stop God from relating to them on the basis of Christ's obedience, and cause Him to draw back from them.

Depending on what level of sin they think overcomes His blood, Christians choose their spiritual home from a range of options running from liberal (more sin-tolerating) through to fundamentalist (less sin-tolerating) practices. The latter tend to look down on the former, much as a man who can jump four feet in the air looks down on one who can only jump two feet, despite the fact that the target height is the stars!

It is not hard to see why the failure to accept that Christ did a complete work on the cross has led the body of Christ dividing many times. Each time a church reaches for the Law to try and curb sin, it takes the eyes of the congregation off the perfect and complete work of Christ and onto the imperfect and incomplete lives of the congregation; a sure recipe to stir up condemnation, judgment, and division, for that is exactly the Law's purpose: to point out fault. (When was the last time you were stopped by the police for good driving?)

But if churches are not supposed to be preaching the Law ("thou shalt not do this and thou better do that") to make Christians lead better lives, then what should they be preaching? The apostle Paul answers that: "…but we preach Christ crucified, to the Jews a stumbling block and to the Greeks foolishness, but to those who are called, both Jews and Greeks, Christ the power of God and the wisdom of God. Because the foolishness of God is wiser than men, and the weakness of God is stronger than men" (1 Corinthians 1:23–25). Notice how Paul names the message preached by the early church that brought the power of God as "Christ crucified." Preaching the gospel as the early church did is about telling people about what God has done for them and His grace, rather than what they need to do for God by following the Law, for here is the good news: what the Law is powerless to do, God did! (Romans 8:3)

Chapter 7

God's solution—a new creation

> "Therefore, if anyone is in Christ, he is a new creation; old things have passed away; behold, all things have become new."
>
> 2 Corinthians 5:17

God's solution to our self-centered hearts has never been for us to try and make our lives holier by merely modifying our behavior (pruning the branches). His solution has always been that nothing short of a heart transplant will do (an entirely new root for an entirely new tree). Through the prophet Ezekiel, who lived five hundred years before Christ, God gave notice of how He intended to deal with the problem of our hard hearts. We could call it His transplant or exchange promise. "I will give you a new heart and put a new spirit within you; I will take the heart of stone out of your flesh and give you a heart of flesh" (Ezekiel 36:26). The very next verse confirms what this new heart is and how we are to receive it: "I will put My Spirit within you and cause you to walk in my statutes, and you will keep my judgments and do them" (Ezekiel 36:27). This prophecy is nothing short of a description of God bringing about a new creation, through the life, death, and resurrection of Jesus.

Let us come back to our picture of an entirely new root for an entirely new tree. Scientists have discovered that each of us receives the DNA code that determines our natural characteristics from our parents. A person's complete set of genetic instructions is called their "genome." Each genome contains all the information needed to build that organism and allow it to function as it should. We could say that our genome both allows us to be who we are and restricts us from being anyone else. Years of research have uncovered the process by which these instructions in the DNA are converted into a living body and scientists have given this fundamental process to natural life a very interesting name. They call it the "Central Dogma." This is a very apt name, as the word "dogma" is our descriptive term for the fundamental beliefs of any religion or ideology, beliefs that are so important that any change to them would cause the very nature of the religion to change.

Just such a fundamental change came upon Adam in the Garden of Eden when he believed the lie of Satan. These days we are familiar with the concept of a virus affecting the programmed operating system of a computer, rendering it incapable of doing what it was originally intended to do. But even this picture is inadequate to describe the fundamental change that took place in Adam when he sinned. This change happened at the very deepest level of his being—his spirit, through which he was in communion with his creator (Genesis 2:17). By choosing to believe what Satan said over what God said, a change took place that redirected his very being, away from his creator, who is Spirit, and down onto the created things, the natural realm. We can see a depiction of this "fall of being" from the spiritual realm down to the natural realm in Romans 1:25, where Paul points back to the cause of people being cut off from God in their sin. "Who changed the truth of God into a lie, and worshiped and served the creature more than the Creator, who is blessed for ever. Amen."

Notice what was changed that resulted in man's separation from God and ultimate death. "Who changed the truth of God into a lie." The truth of God was Adam's spiritual genome. God's truth and life are one. Jesus revealed this union when He declared, "I am the Way, the Truth and the Life" (John 14:6). If truth and life are so connected, we can see that each life develops as the product of the truth (genome) that a man lives by (Proverbs 23:7). In each life there runs a Central Dogma, producing life from the truth that is in a man (Matthew 6:21–23). There is no escaping the power of dogma in our lives. Our very lives will be born out of the truth we believe (Luke 6:45).

Adam was unique in that, being the first man from whom all others would come, whatever befell Adam affected all of mankind. This is illustrated in the fact that although Eve ate the forbidden fruit first, her condition did not change until Adam (her spiritual head) also ate (Genesis 3:6–7). When the source of a river is poisoned, everything downstream is affected. Adam was a "type" of Christ (Romans 5:14, 1 Corinthians 15:45) in that he prefigured someone who was greater than him. He was a shadow of a greater reality. Just as being the first of a new race, whatever happened to the first Adam affected us all, because we were born of him, so whatever happened to the last Adam (Christ) would also affect everyone born of Him (Romans 5:12–21, 1 Corinthians 15:20–28). "And so it is written, 'The first man Adam was made a living soul;' the last Adam was made a quickening spirit"[23] (1 Corinthians 15:45).

Just as Satan came to tempt the first Adam, he also came to tempt the last Adam, but where the first Adam fell, the last Adam triumphed (Romans 5:17). Listen to the words of Jesus when Satan comes to him in the desert to tempt Him to disbelieve God and thus change the truth of God into a lie. First the devil offers Jesus an alternative

---

[23] King James Version.

view of reality, a different truth to live by: that God is not His source of life and that He must become His own source of life through what He does. Notice this is the same lie the first Adam was told.

> "Then Jesus was led by the Spirit into the wilderness to be tempted by the devil. After fasting forty days and forty nights, he was hungry. The tempter came to him and said, 'If you are the Son of God, tell these stones to become bread.'
>
> Jesus answered, 'It is written: 'Man shall not live on bread alone, but on every word that comes from the mouth of God''."[24] (Matthew 4:1–4)

Here Jesus is declaring that the source of a man's life, the root from which all else grows, is the truth that remains in Him (the truth he believes). A man's "heart," or inner person, is the source of his feelings, decisions and actions. Everything he is arises from what he has accepted as truth and the truth that has remained in him. Knowing this principle immediately alerts us to the importance of receiving the truth about life and guarding that truth as our very lives. This warning is given in Proverbs 4:23, "Keep your heart with all diligence, for out of it spring the issues of life." In other words, our hearts—the truth we believe—are the wellspring from which all the issues of our lives flow. The Hebrew word, translated here as "issues," literally means the outer border or extremity. What we believe determines and sets the limits and the borders of our lives. None of us can live beyond what we have believed. If I believe in my heart that I am worthless as a person, then no matter how much money, fame, or how many friends I accumulate, I will live in inner poverty, for what I have believed imprisons me. The only way I can be free is if a more powerful truth comes to me; one that will

---

[24] New International Version.

reveal what I had thought of as true to be a lie. This truth effectively dethrones the lie that ruled me and sets me free to live an entirely new life, out of an entirely new genome (a new tree from a new seed).

The most powerful truth in the world, the truth that dethrones every other "truth" and makes all men who will receive Him free, is Christ! Jesus declared, "And ye shall know the truth, and the truth shall make you free"[25] (John 8:32).

The truth is that where the first Adam failed, the last Adam succeeded. The truth of what Christ has done for us, that He has become our new root and our genome for an entirely new life, sets our hearts free from the limitations of the life we inherited from Adam, a life bordered and imprisoned by sin and death. The same life and the same Spirit that broke Christ out of the prison of death is the same life that now remains in everyone who receives Christ as their new life. It isn't enough to say that a Christian is someone who receives Christ *into* their life. A Christian is someone who has received Christ *as* their life (Colossians 3:4). God is not in the business of fixing up the old tree. He has replaced the root system to produce an entirely new tree! The first Adam was a living soul, but to be born of the last Adam is to be born of a "life-giving Spirit" (1 Corinthians 15:45).

The life we were born into and lived out of the first Adam was separated from God and destined to perish. The life we now live out of the last Adam (Christ) was born out of a new seed; it is an eternal, abundant life, because it is a life sourced from our union with an eternal, abundant God (1 Corinthians 6:17). We received this life as our new life when we heard and believed the gospel. By the grace of God, our hearts were the good soil in which the supernatural seed of the Word of God, the truth, and the life of Christ, was implanted and now dwells. "For you have been born again, not of perishable

---

[25] King James Version.

seed, but of imperishable, through the living and enduring word of God"[26] (1 Peter 1:23).

Christ is now God's view and opinion of us and when we start to live from this truth and abide in it, then we find that Jesus's promise is true; His life does indeed start to manifest in our lives. "Abide in Me, and I in you. As the branch cannot bear fruit of itself, unless it abides in the vine, neither can you, unless you abide in Me. I am the vine, you are the branches. He who abides in Me, and I in him, bears much fruit; for without Me you can do nothing" (John 15:4–5).

Once again, this promise speaks not of us changing ourselves and our behavior from the outside in, but of God Himself exchanging our hearts and making us new from the inside out by giving us His own nature. So what is God's nature?

> "God is a Spirit: and they that worship him must worship him in spirit and in truth." (John 4:24)

Words are insufficient to adequately describe God's nature, but from His own Word we know that God is Spirit (John 4:24), God is love (1 John 4:8), and God is holy (1 Peter 1:16). This is what the "life" of God is and so to know His nature in you is to know His eternal life in you (John 17:3). We also know that God desires that all men and women should receive His life, so that they would be one with Him. This is the good news that Jesus declared in His often-quoted words recorded in John 3:16, "For God so loved the world that He gave His only begotten Son, that whoever believes in Him should not perish but have everlasting life."

On the night before He died, Jesus, in His prayer to the Father, declared again the purpose of His coming and the reason why He would die on the cross, "…that they may be one just as We are one:

---

[26] New International Version.

I in them, and You in Me; that they may be made perfect in one, and that the world may know that You have sent Me, and have loved them as You have loved Me" (John 17:22–23).

Jesus declared that the Father loves us, just as He loves His own Son. He also told us that just as we express our love to our children by lavishing gifts on them, so God desires to express His love for His children by pouring into our lives all we need to live a blessed and generous life (Matthew 7:11). Such a life glorifies and reveals the generosity of our Father to this world (Matthew 5:16). Contrary to popular thinking, salvation is all about what God has done for us, not about what we need to do for Him. It is all about His grace, for if our salvation were the result of something we had done, that could not be grace (Romans 11:6, Galatians 3:10–13).

Chapter 8

Like Father like sons

> "That which is born of the flesh is flesh, and that which is born of the Spirit is spirit. Do not marvel that I said to you, 'You must be born again'."
>
> John 3:6–7

Now we see the reason why our old sinful life was exchanged on the cross for Jesus's perfect life. This is exactly what Jesus prayed for, "that they may be made perfect in one" (John 17:23). By placing us in the life of His Son, the Father is able to relate to us and we to Him, just as He relates to Jesus. With sin no longer a barrier between us and the Father, we are able to access the same grace, the same power, and the same authority that Jesus lived in during His earthly ministry. This is why Jesus was able to leave His disciples with the commission to heal the sick and raise the dead, and assure them that they would do all He did and more. This promise is recorded in John 14:12: "Most assuredly, I say to you, he who believes in Me, the works that I do he will do also; and greater works than these he will do, because I go to My Father."

Christians healing the sick is one of the signs that the good news is true, that our sin really has been dealt with, and that now the same

Spirit who rose Christ from the dead is living in every Christian (Romans 8:11). The early church knew this truth and the people lived lives of great power and authority in Christ (Acts 3:6). Despite being viciously persecuted, the early church was able to flourish and overcome the Roman Empire because its message that God had completely dealt with man's sin continued to be confirmed as Jesus promised it would, with miraculous healings and salvation (Mark 16:15–18). Even Jesus did not expect His message to be believed without such signs accompanying His teaching (John 10:37–38), so what right do we have to expect people to listen to us without such signs? Are we better preachers than He was?

The book of Hebrews was written to people who had been trying to make themselves right with God for many years the old way (through their own obedience to the Laws of God). It was written to show them that the Old Covenant had failed to make them holy as God is holy, but the New Covenant had now achieved this, therefore making the old way "obsolete." "In that He says, 'A new covenant,' He has made the first obsolete. Now what is becoming obsolete and growing old is ready to vanish away" (Hebrews 8:13).

The Law can still be used today to reveal to non-Christians their sin and their inability to defeat it. The high moral standards demanded by God's commandments still serve as a schoolmaster to lead people to the conclusion that they need a Savior (Galatians 3:24). But Christians are not to operate under that system any more (Galatians 1:6–8). Once you are in Christ, trying to make yourself holy by keeping the commandments is like attempting to use Windows 95 on the latest laptop. New creations cannot work with obsolete operating systems!

Trying to make Christians holier by using the Law to point out their sin, in the hope that they will try harder to be holy, is to deny what Christ accomplished on the cross. He did not just forgive our sins and leave us to try harder to improve our lives with the help of the Law and the Spirit; He ended our lives!

As Christians, our old life of "try harder to be holy, fail, repent, and try again" died on the cross and was buried with Christ (Romans 6:2–6, 7:6). In exchange we got the sinless, perfected life of Christ, which is why the Word of God can declare that, as believers, we rose with Him and are now seated with Him in heavenly places. Listen to how Paul declares this truth to the Ephesians:

> "But God, who is rich in mercy, because of His great love with which He loved us, even when we were dead in trespasses, made us alive together with Christ (by grace you have been saved), and raised us up together, and made us sit together in the heavenly places in Christ Jesus, that in the ages to come He might show the exceeding riches of His grace in His kindness toward us in Christ Jesus. For by grace you have been saved through faith, and that not of yourselves; it is the gift of God, not of works, lest anyone should boast." (Ephesians 2:4–9)

This is the powerful declaration that our water baptism makes of our new victorious life in Christ; a life of faith in Him. Water baptism declares that He has indeed already done all that is necessary to place us in eternal life and to place eternal life in us. In the natural realm, if someone dies, we do not leave the body lying around, but do the decent thing and bury it. So, too, our baptism is our opportunity to publicly declare to ourselves, to our community, and to Satan that through faith in Christ the old "try harder to be holy" me is dead and to hold a funeral service for that old man.

This is what being laid down below the waters declares: that we were buried with Christ. Being immediately lifted up out of the waters declares the reason and the effect of our death and burial with Him. It is in order that we could rise in Him to lead a new victorious life, united, at one with God, no longer under the old system of trying to deal with our own sin, but perfected in Christ, with access through faith to the entire blessing of the heavenly realm. That is exactly how Paul greeted the Ephesians at the start of his letter to them, "Blessed be the God and Father of our Lord Jesus Christ, who has blessed us with every spiritual blessing in the heavenly places in Christ" (Ephesians 1:3). Note the use of the past tense: He *has blessed* us with all that heaven has. Now we are equipped to be the answer to the Lord's prayer: "Let your kingdom come, your will be done, on earth as it is in heaven"[27] (Matthew 6:10).

The evidence of the kingdom is the manifestation of the authority and power of the King. Jesus did not expect His disciples to preach about the kingdom of God without the evidence of that authority and power in their lives. "And heal the sick there, and say to them, 'The kingdom of God has come near to you'" (Luke 10:9).

There is no lack, no sickness, and no sin in heaven. It should be obvious, then, to those of us who have prayed all our lives, "let thy kingdom come on earth as it is in heaven," that it is God's will that the life of a Christian reflect heaven. In the same way that His life in us bears in us the fruit of holiness, so, too, His life in us should reveal His kingdom not to be powerless in the area of sickness or poverty. This does not mean that we "chase after" health and wealth, but rather that we believe and therefore live in the truth that Jesus declared in Matthew 7:11 that our Father in heaven is a generous giver, even more than any of us would be with our own children. Our faith is not about moving the hand of God to bless us. He is not a neglectful father who must be coaxed into caring for his children. Rather, He is so generous that, through the cross, He has freely

---

[27] New International Version.

provided access to the abundance of His generous life to all who will believe Him to be who He is: a generous loving Father.

A heart that is persuaded that Father God is generous remains persuaded in every season, whether we appear to have plenty or not. "I know what it is to be in need, and I know what it is to have plenty. I have learned the secret of being content in any and every situation, whether well fed or hungry, whether living in plenty or in want"[28] (Philippians 4:12).

Faith is not a work that moves the hand of God to give. Despite what you may have heard, neither does your financial giving. We may have learned in this world how to move or manipulate people to be good to us through giving to them, but to teach that we can move God by giving to Him is to reduce God to the level of a man and will ultimately harden our hearts toward Him (Acts 17:25). The God of whom the gospel speaks loves us so much that He found a way to free us from striving to earn His blessing. At just the right time, when we were powerless to earn His love, He gave us everything He had (Romans 5:6). Live in that truth and you will find rest for your soul. You will find your daily bread and the faith to leave tomorrow up to Him.

To believe that my faith can move God would be placing my hope in my faith, instead of in Christ. Such faith would bring me no peace, for the object of my hope would have fallen off Christ and back onto myself! True faith rests; it does not strive. Faith in Christ is faith in *His* life, *His* performance, and *His* holiness, not mine. In fact, biblical faith is not "of ourselves" at all, but is a gift from God (Ephesians 2:8–9), a gift that comes through hearing Christ's words (John 6:63). Faith enables us to take hold of what God has already

---

[28] New International Version.

provided through the cross, not take hold of God's arm to twist it to provide more!

What causes faith to arise in us is the revelation of the magnitude of the grace and generosity of God (Romans 10:14–17). It is no wonder the apostle Paul prayed that his beloved Ephesians would have their eyes opened more fully to the provision already available (Ephesians 3:17–19). What produces holiness and faith in our lives is nothing short of the nature of Christ and the Spirit of God dwelling in us (Galatians 5:22). Just as a seed grows best in undisturbed soil, the fruit of His Spirit will blossom best in our lives as our faith rests ever more in what He has done, rather than in what we can do (Galatians 3:2–5). Our diligence to study, believe, and pray the promises of God are not in order to merit God's blessing, but to renew our religious minds to an awesome truth—that through the finished work of Christ we can now partake in the nature of God and enjoy fellowship with the Father, Son, and Holy Spirit (2 Peter 1:3–5). The primary work of the Holy Spirit is to convince us, not of what we need to do, but of what Christ has done (Romans 8:16), and to lead us into this new way of living. "I am crucified with Christ: nevertheless I live; yet not I, but Christ liveth in me: and the life which I now live in the flesh I live by the faith of the Son of God, who loved me, and gave himself for me"[29] (Galatians 2:20).

Jesus is the author and finisher of our faith (Hebrews 12:2). As believers, the source and the substance of our faith is found in Him and the good news of the gospel is that He is found in us! (1 John 4:4) So it is by *His* faith that we are living *His* life (Galatians 2:20). Note that Paul says that he lives by the faith *of* the Son of God. If the faith that saves us is a gift from Him, rather than something we must work up from within us, can you see how much of a burden

---

[29] King James Version.

is lifted off us, for this truth lifts our eyes off *our* performance and back onto Christ's.

It is Christ living *in* us that saves us, not our efforts living *for* Him. It is beholding Him (His faith) that brings about our transformation into His likeness (2 Corinthians 3:18), not beholding ourselves (our faith). Any teaching that appears to direct our hope back onto our own performance ("if only you had more faith") has just pointed us away from the source of power to live as He did, and from His grace (divine influence). Scripture clearly declares that the life that saves us is "not from yourselves." The faith that saves us cannot be from us, for that would mean that we have been able to work up the power to be saved from within ourselves and therefore have something to boast about. But what does the gospel say about such boasting? "For it is by grace you have been saved, through faith—and this is not from yourselves, it is the gift of God—not by works, so that no one can boast"[30] (Ephesians 2:8).

We have all been given "the measure" (*metron*) (Strong's G3358) of faith (Romans 12:3) and that measure is Christ (Ephesians 4:13). Comparing our faith with that of others can be a sign that we still have not realized that all who have received Christ have been given "like precious faith" (2 Peter 1:1). The phrase "like precious" is the translation of the Greek word *isotimus*, which means "of equal value" (Strong's G2472).

Since it is not our faith that justifies us, but the faith of He who saved us, we are not called to try to believe God out of our own self-generated version of faith. There is only one type of faith that saves us: God's faith. Man's natural inherent ability to believe something is not defined by the Bible as faith, or else there would be millions of different types of faith. Yet what does Ephesians 4:4–6 declare?

---

[30] New International Version.

"There is one body, and one Spirit, even as ye are called in one hope of your calling. One Lord, one faith, one baptism, One God and Father of all, who is above all, and through all, and in you all."[31]

We are only able to believe God because of this one faith, the faith of Jesus Christ, gifted to us through His Word (Romans 10:17) and working in us by His Holy Spirit (1 Corinthians 12:3). Only by His faith and His Spirit can we can begin to see what God sees and what we see transforms our lives!

> "Therefore, from now on, we regard no one according to the flesh." (2 Corinthians 5:16)

Seeing by the Spirit shows us what the Spirit sees. He sees you as the object of the Father's love, worth giving His Son for, and speaks to you accordingly—graciously and lovingly. Ministering to believers in the power of the Spirit, we no longer regard them or relate to them according to whom the world sees them to be, but whom the Father sees them to be. The most life-changing truth to minister to a young believer is not that they need to be holier, but that they are holy! (1 Corinthians 6:11) Because of the lack of understanding of their righteousness under the New Covenant, so many believers remain spiritual infants (Hebrews 5:13). If He wants His children to grow up and take their positions of responsibility, a good father knows that there comes a time when he must stop treating them as children. Continuing to minister the Law to believers is like treating them as infants, or as people without faith (Galatians 3:12). But the truth is that they have been given the faith *of* Christ (Galatians 2:16), so that they would no longer need the schoolmaster of the Law (Galatians 3:24). The great danger in ministers not speaking to believers according to who they are in the Spirit, but in continuing to relate to them in the soulish realm, is that they never grow up

---

[31] King James Version.

into their new identity as sons, but remain as infants tossed to and fro by their circumstances, perceiving only in the natural realm (1 Corinthians 2:14, Ephesians 4:14). If they remain unrenewed in their minds to the spiritual truth of their new position in Christ, they will live as chickens when they have been called to live as eagles! There is a great need in the body of Christ for fathers who can recognize maturity and to call others into its redeemed liberty.

Stand firm, then, in the exalted position that Christ died to lift you into. Remain in the revelation of your communion with Him. Remain living in the Spirit and do not let men, blinded by the glory of their own sacrifices, lure you back to the dry and fruitless fields of religion, with great promises of fruit to come. It sounds like such an innocent request to add just a little of your own holiness to Christ's work. But just as a snare looks like a feeble piece of wire compared to the strength of a wild animal, nevertheless it will kill it, for it is the very strength of the animal's own struggles that will tighten the noose and choke the life of the blood. Do not be so easily ensnared (Galatians 5:1). That little lie, that if you only tried a little harder to please God then He would bless you, has choked the life and joy of salvation from countless believers who are left crying out to God to restore to them the joy that they themselves give away.

Only someone who cannot see the riches of grace already his in Christ would estrange himself from the Father (Luke 15:29–31). Let His grace be sufficient for you and you will find that His grace will teach you and empower you to deny ungodliness in a way your natural strength never could (Titus 2:11–13, Colossians 2:23). Let the revelation of His grace—of how He has exalted you in Christ—humble you, so that you are able to speak to others with His gentleness (Matthew 11:29). Be careful to give Him all the glory for His life in you, for to give people the impression that it was your faith that saved you, not His gift, would point them in the wrong direction. The gospel of grace only points to one life and declares that we all have that same life, so that no one can boast, which leads to division (1 Corinthians 3:18–23).

The good news we have for this nation and this world is that our Father in heaven loves us so much that He never wanted the gift of His life to be dependent on something as fragile and weak as our willpower. He never intended for His children to live ashamed before Him, trying to cover over their sin with the fig leaves of their own best efforts. The Law wasn't given so that we could attempt to cover ourselves in glory, but so we could see the glory that was missing (Romans 3:23). The commandments of God were not given so that man could overcome sin, but so that he could see how completely sin had overcome him and separated him from the glory of God (Romans 3:19). God's answer to our separation has always been union with Him, accomplished entirely by Him, for this is who He has always truly been; the Father who withholds nothing from us, even His own life (Luke 15:12, Romans 8:32).

If you can understand that God is not asking you to produce fruit, but to bear fruit, then you have understood the gospel of grace. We cannot be the root or the source of godliness in our lives. He is the root and the vine and we are the branches (John 15:5). The Christian life is *His* life, the life of God in man. It is a resurrected, ascended, overcoming, reigning life. Best of all it is the "together" life (Ephesians 2:4–8). When we were dead in our sins and powerless to help ourselves, He made us alive "together with Christ." He "raised us up together" and made us sit "together in Christ" in the heavenly realms. This "together with God" life, or "in-Christ" life, is the gift that fully reveals the exceeding richness of the grace of God toward man. It is fully expressed through individual lives as they live, not alone, but together with others, giving freely the grace they have received (Ephesians 4:13–16). Every local fellowship of believers is called to witness to their community through the harmony of their lives together, showing that the real high life is about community and not individuality (John 13:35).

The best way any believer can allow the grace of God to be revealed through his life is to live from the exalted position of union with God that Christ died to place him in. To do that, we must leave behind the schoolmaster of the Law and take up the privilege and responsibility of sonship. We must take our place in the Father's house and at the table He has prepared for us, for truly the grace of God enables us to be everything He always saw us to be: partakers in the eternal life of the Trinity (John 17:20–26). By the grace of God, may His Spirit open our eyes to see ourselves as He sees us, so that we may live the life He made us to enjoy; the life of Immanuel, God with us (Matthew 1:23).

Chapter 9

Church growth...the apostolic way

> "And He Himself gave some to be apostles, some prophets, some evangelists, and some pastors and teachers, for the equipping of the saints for the work of ministry, for the edifying of the body of Christ, till we all come to the unity of the faith and of the knowledge of the Son of God, to a perfect man, to the measure of the stature of the fullness of Christ."
>
> Ephesians 4:11–13

Again and again, the scriptures declare the faith of Jesus not just to be a model for us to try and emulate, but to be the actual instrument of our salvation, so that ALL the glory goes to Jesus for our salvation, for it is ALL by His gift of grace (Romans 11:6).

Knowing this wonderful truth that even the faith we need has been gifted to us enables our hearts to enter a state of resting more completely in Christ, as the revelation of His love for us grows in us (Matthew 11:28). In fact it is through the fruit of His love growing in us that His faith is expressed through us (Galatians 5:6) and the effect of this revelation in His body is unity (Ephesians 4:13–15). We can finally grow out of the immaturity of comparing ourselves with ourselves and church with church, which has only led to division in the body (1 Corinthians 1:11–13, 2 Corinthians 10:12).

So much division has been caused by Christians focusing on how they differ in what they are doing for God, comparing one believer's faith, or one church's works, with that of another. Yet Ephesians 4 tells us that only the spiritual growth of individual believers in the reality of their union with Christ will lead to a manifestation of unity across the body of Christ, for true spiritual growth is about growing together into one perfect man (Ephesians 4:13).

So let us not fall back into religion or into trying to manipulate God through our prayers or works to give us more faith. Let us discover the truth of His Word, that faith actually flows in and through us as we begin to acknowledge every good thing that has *already* been placed in us (Philemon 1:6). This revelation of the unity of one faith and that our stature as a believer is nothing other than the fullness of Christ, is ministered to the saints (the body of Christ) by the ascension ministry gifts Jesus placed in His Church. These are identified in Ephesians 4 as apostle, prophet, evangelist, pastor, and teacher. This is the apostolic blueprint for true church growth; a growth in the revelation of Christ as our life and the manifestation of that revelation in the body, as the glory and nature of Christ in His people. Only this revelation of Christ as our one new life leads to true unity of heart and mind, as we grow up together into this one new man (Ephesians 4:11–16). Without such spiritual growth, churches may appear to grow numerically, but shallow roots make for shallow lives. Oak trees do not grow overnight, but their strength is founded on the depth of their roots. Let Christ be our root in all things, especially faith, and we will find ourselves experiencing His vision of church growth; the ever-growing fruit of His Spirit in us (John 15:5), and a unity of spirit across the church that speaks to the world of one life (John 13:35).

God never asks us to do anything that His life in us doesn't want to do or isn't able to do. In truth, He never asks us to do anything but what His life in us can do, for He is convinced that we are, and wants us to be, a totally new creation, joined to Him in Spirit, and to have within us the same miracle-working spirit that rose Christ from the dead. If I want my children to be convinced of their worth in my eyes, then I refuse point blank to address them in any other way except in the truth of their worth. Even if they feel badly about themselves, I refuse to speak to them in agreement with the way they feel, but want my words to lift them up into the truth of their great worth.

Please listen carefully. Even though we may struggle to see ourselves as one with God in spirit, supernatural children of a supernatural God, our Father cannot agree to speak to us according to how we feel. He cannot speak a lie. This is why the things the Holy Spirit says to His church will appear to natural soulish thinking as foolishness, whereas the things that a mere religious spirit would teach appear quite reasonable. Have you never noticed that religion only asks of you what is possible? It will tell you: pray more, do more, give more; all of which are possible and appeal to the "me" life that asks what can I do *for* God. But the Holy Spirit does not speak to believers of the possible, but of the impossible. He says, "Heal the sick, raise the dead, cleanse those who have leprosy, drive out demons. Freely you have received; freely give"[32] (Matthew 10:8).

Why? Why does the Holy Spirit ask of believers things which, without God's Spirit, are impossible to do? Because He can see clearly what we have not yet seen. As believers, we are NOT apart from the Spirit of God, but are one Spirit with Him. The life He has called us to is NOT a natural "do-your-best-for-God" life. It is "God's-best-in-you" life. The Holy Spirit does not speak to the

---

[32] New International Version.

"me" life. He speaks to the "us" life (1 Corinthians 6:19). When we teach Christians that rather than pray to God for the sick, that they should heal the sick, many actually get offended that we are asking the impossible of them! The ironic thing is that when we look across the body of Christ, what we see is many Christians getting burnt out, not by trying to do the impossible, but by trying to do nothing but the possible and striving to do it better! God asks us to do the impossible, for that is who He insists we now are: people yoked to the God of the impossible, a people who have ceased striving toward their "possible" works, and a people who have found rest in allowing His life in them—the impossibly good life—to be their life. Scripture warns us to be careful what belief we yoke our lives to. "Stand fast therefore in the liberty by which Christ has made us free, and do not be entangled again with a yoke of bondage" (Galatians 5:1).

This one verse sums up the purpose of the apostle Paul's letter to the Galatians. The "yoke of bondage" was Paul's description of the trap or snare of trying to earn the favor and blessing of God through our own performance. When man tries to make himself righteous in God's eyes through his own efforts, we can generally give that mindset a name: religion! Paul was in effect saying, "Don't get entangled in religion." The Greek word translated here as "entangled" is based on the picture of being ensnared. The danger of a snare is found in its deceptive appearance. It looks insignificant and yet can inflict fatal damage. As a vet I would sometimes treat animals who had been caught in a snare and often they would have to be put to sleep. In its simplest form, a snare is a loop of wire or strong string that closes around the neck or limb of an animal as it runs through it. It may not look very threatening, but the more the victim struggles to get free of a snare, the tighter the noose cuts into it. Put a small loop of wire beside a strong animal and it looks no match for its strength. It looks insignificant. But the cruel thing about a snare is that it is not the strength of the snare that kills the animal, it is the strength of the animal, for what tightens the snare is the struggle of the victim. The more it uses its own strength to try and get free, the tighter it is caught in the snare's hold.

Multitudes of people across different faith systems and even across Christian churches are caught in the snare of religion; the little idea that we can get more from God by behaving better. Once caught in this snare, people can struggle for a lifetime, repeatedly offering up to God the strength of their devotions to Him, not realizing that their best efforts to earn something from him are like the struggles of the animal in the snare. All their efforts are doing is choking the effect of the grace of God in their lives (Galatians 5:4). This is because grace and truth are inseparable (John 1:14), and the truth that they are distancing themselves from is that God has already freely given us all we need to live a godly life (Romans 8:32, 2 Peter 1:3), for what greater gift can He give but His Son and His Spirit?

If we approach God as if we can cajole blessings out of Him through the quality of our devotions, it is like approaching Him blind to who He really is and to what He has already given (Luke 15:28–31). The work of the Holy Spirit is to open our eyes to the reality that God sees and the enormity of what has already been freely given to us in the gift of Christ (1 Corinthians 2:12).

If He already gave us the best that He had to give when we had done nothing to deserve such love (Romans 5:8), what makes us think that He now relates to us on the basis of what we deserve? When did He change His mind? I believe this is why the Holy Spirit prompted Paul to use that picture of being ensnared when speaking of trying to earn the approval of God through your actions. Paul was trying to warn the Galatians that once they started back down the road of trying to make themselves righteous through their actions, the noose of the Law and performance to a certain standard would rapidly tighten around them and effectively choke the power of God in their lives (Galatians 3:2–5). That's what he meant when he declared later in Galatians 5:9, "a little leaven leavens the whole lump." Paul was effectively saying, "It may seem like a harmless thing to you now, this little idea that you can wrestle more blessing from God by behaving better. It may seem beneficial, but it will take a vice-like grip of your life. This idea will grow to consume you, until everything you do becomes all about you and what you are doing for God, instead of about God and what He has done for you" (1 John 4:10). You will have fallen from God-consciousness into self-consciousness and will live more aware of the weakness of your life *for* God than of the strength of His life *in* you. Your life will have become ensnared by religion.

Paul's letter to the Galatians is one of the most passionate defenses ever composed of what he knew as "the gospel of God's grace" (Acts 20:24). He believed that adding the smallest man-made requirement to the simplicity of Christ's message would corrupt the gospel entirely (2 Corinthians 11:3). He felt this so strongly that his opening remarks to the Galatians begin with a stinging rebuke for anyone who would dare to preach a gospel other than the one he had first brought to them (Galatians 1:8–9).

What disturbed him so much was that he believed the Galatians had been seduced (Galatians 3:1) from their pure faith in Christ through a perversion of the gospel (Galatians 1:7). False teachers had told them that faith in Christ alone wasn't enough for salvation and that they must also keep requirements of the Old Testament Law, specifically the rite of circumcision. He wrote to exhort them to "stand fast in the liberty" that Christ had won for them and not to be lured back into the dead end of religious performance (Galatians 5:1).

What a shock this letter must have been to the Galatians. They thought that God would be pleased with the sacrifice of circumcision that they were making for Him. That is what some Jewish Christians had been telling them and yet now Paul declared to them, "You have become estranged from Christ, you who attempt to be justified by law; you have fallen from grace" (Galatians 5:4). The King James translation says "Christ has become of no effect unto you," and the Amplified translation reads, "You have been severed from Christ, if you seek to be justified [that is, declared free of the guilt of sin and its penalty, and placed in right standing with God] through the Law; you have fallen from grace [for you have lost your grasp on God's unmerited favour and blessing]." The Galatians, by seeking to justify themselves before God and earn His favor through their righteous acts, had ended up separating themselves and cutting themselves off from the flow of God's grace into their lives.

But surely God wants us to try and please Him? It is the most natural thing in the world for us to try and do our best for God and to seek His blessing on our lives. How could our best efforts to please God be of no effect and leave us hindering His grace in our lives? This is an important question, for finding the answer will save us a lifetime of wasted effort and frustration. How can it be that all my best efforts to please God and earn His blessing may only leave me estranged from His grace? The answer is this: he can't take pleasure in our efforts to earn more of His blessing when such efforts only demonstrate that we have not believed the gospel!

The gospel in fact declares that God can't love us any more than He already does and He can't give us any more than He already has. For by giving us His Son, Jesus, He gave us *everything* He had to give, for what more is there than Christ?

Romans 8:32 sums this up beautifully: "He who did not spare His own Son, but delivered Him up for us all, how shall He not with Him also freely give us all things?" Notice it says that Christ brought "all things," which Peter describes as "everything we need for a godly life" (2 Peter 1:3). In his letter to the Ephesians, Paul affirms that through the gift of Christ, we have been blessed "in the heavenly realms with every spiritual blessing in Christ"[33] (Ephesians 1:3). Note also that this is all in the past tense. Just as wrongly reading a bus timetable may leave you waiting for a bus that has already passed, not understanding what God has already done leaves so many people spending their lives waiting for what has already arrived (Hebrews 10:11–18).

Not only has He given us all that He has, even Christ, but He did it, not when we were on our best behavior, but when we were at our worst! Romans 5:8 declares that through the cross, God demonstrated how radically different His love is from ours, for "God demonstrates his own love for us in this: While we were still sinners, Christ died for us."[34] At the very time in our lives when we were totally incapable of pleasing Him, He gave us the greatest gift, and held nothing of Himself back from us.

God provided the most powerful evidence possible to destroy the lie sown into man; the lie that He is a God who withholds Himself from man (Genesis 3:1–5). Through the life, death, and resurrection of Jesus, the truth about God's unconditional love for man has been established forever (John 3:16). This was done in the most public way possible (Acts 26:26), and the news of it carried across the world so that all people who are in ignorance of who God really is can believe in the God whom Christ revealed; the good Father (John 14:9). Through believing in Him, they find a remarkable thing happening: His character, goodness, and life start to grow in them (Galatians 5:22–23), for their lives were designed for God and apart from Him they have not really experienced life in all its fullness; a life without fear (Hebrews 2:15).

---

[33] New International Version.
[34] New International Version.

He can't bless our efforts to justify ourselves or to make ourselves righteous because that would make salvation about *our* righteousness, but it is not; it is all about *His* righteousness. No matter how many religious sacrifices man makes for God, God cannot agree to begin to make our salvation about our lives given for Him, when it has always been entirely about His life freely given for us (1 Corinthians 2:12).

Paul was distressed for the Galatians because he had learned something that they did not realize: that the power of the gospel is found in living by what God has done for you, not by what you are doing for Him (2 Corinthians 3:18). The moment we start to emphasize what we are doing for Him, we turn away from the source of our strength and the joy of the truth that He has done all that is necessary for our salvation (John 19:30). Unfortunately when we dress up the emphasis on our performance with terms like "holiness unto the Lord," "obedience," or even "faith," we obscure the true foundation of a Christian's new life, which is Christ's holiness, obedience, and faith. Only what emerges from that foundation in our lives will stand the test of eternity (1 Corinthians 3:10–15).

Chapter 10

Religion versus the gospel

"This is love: not that we loved God, but that he loved us and sent his Son as an atoning sacrifice for our sins."[35]

1 John 4:10

When we first became Christians, there was nothing that we brought to merit our own salvation. We were totally incapable of doing anything to earn salvation. In fact, this truth is what prepares our hearts to receive Christ; we come to the place of realizing that good works, prayer, and going to church will never change our hard, self-centered hearts. We need a Savior to rescue us (Ephesians 2:8). Perhaps while reading this book you find yourself in that place for the first time. After constantly trying to change yourself, you have come to the place of knowing that your best efforts will never be good enough to make you right with God, that you can't save yourself, and that you need a Savior. That place is called the cross.

Or maybe you are a Christian and over the years you seem to have lost the joy of your salvation and you can't understand why. Could it be that you, too, need to come back to this place, to see what you

---
[35] New International Version.

saw at first; that what Jesus did for you on the cross is 100% enough to save you. It cannot be anything less than 100% Jesus's work, for even if it were 99% His work and the rest yours, how would you ever know with certainty that you had managed your 1%? After a lifetime of religion, you would reach your deathbed still in doubt over your salvation. That would be living far short of the boldness and assurance the gospel promises us (Ephesians 4:11–14, Hebrews 4:16, 10:22, James 1:6).

At the very beginning of our Christian walk, our new life was all about what Christ had done for us. Paul was declaring to the Galatians that their new life should *remain* all about what He had done for them. We were never meant to move on from that truth, as if Jesus was the author and we should be the finisher of our salvation. He is both the Alpha and the Omega (Revelation 22:13, Hebrews 12:2). If Jesus is your Savior, then let His grace and His life in you *be* your salvation (John 15:5). Paul said the same thing to the Colossians. "As you therefore have received Christ Jesus the Lord, so walk in Him" (Colossians 2:6). But can you remember how we received Christ as our new life?

We received Him by believing the gospel of His grace; by believing that He was generous enough to give Himself completely to us (Ephesians 2:8). That remains exactly how we continue to walk with Him as children of God; by faith in His grace, a faith that is gifted to us (Romans 10:17) and makes us righteous, apart from the Law (Romans 3:20–24). The gospel message declares that no matter how hard we try or how much we sacrifice, God can't bless our efforts to justify ourselves or to make ourselves righteous, because would to make salvation about *our* righteousness, when in truth it is all about *His* righteousness.

That truth should give you more joy than anything else you will ever hear, for, despite what every religious sermon you have ever heard has tried to tell you, God has never expected any of us to be the source of goodness or godliness in our own lives! The original lie of Satan in the Garden of Eden is still a lie (Genesis 3:4–5). The knowledge of good and evil is not enough to make us like God, for it is only by receiving His life (like the fruit of the tree of life) that we can be like Him. The only good life is God's life and it is a life received, not a life achieved! A wonderful passage of scripture that illustrates this great truth is Romans 3:21–26.

> "But now the righteousness of God apart from the law is revealed, being witnessed by the Law and the Prophets, even the righteousness of God, through faith in Jesus Christ, to all and on all who believe. For there is no difference; for all have sinned and fall short of the glory of God, being justified freely by His grace through the redemption that is in Christ Jesus, whom God set forth as a propitiation by His blood, through faith, to demonstrate *His righteousness*, because in His forbearance God had passed over the sins that were previously committed, to demonstrate at the present time *His righteousness*, that He might be just and the justifier of the one who has faith in Jesus." (emphasis added)

Here we see why God can't bless our efforts to earn His blessing through what we do. The answer is declared twice in this passage, both times in the same phrase; "to demonstrate His righteousness," not ours! We always want to make things about us. When we do that, we get in the way of the flow of the grace of God in our lives. Religion (the belief that we can move God by our piety) inevitably moves our hope from what God has done for us (given Christ) and toward what we have done for Him (self-effort).

The confusing thing is that religion sounds and looks so attractive. We are told that, in effect, our lives are a disappointment to God, but there are some disciplines that we can carry out that will cause Him to change His mind about us and bless us more. We just have to pray enough, give enough, and work hard enough at changing ourselves and when God sees that we are doing enough, then He will bless us by allowing us to share in His life. This sounds right and feels right, because to our own eyes, our failures are always before us and the idea that we could influence God and move Him appeals to our pride. Without the Holy Spirit, man remains helpless in the face of the demands of religion, because in his own eyes, he agrees with religion's accusations and exhortations to try harder. What sets a man free is the gift of the Holy Spirit and the ability to see himself through God's eyes (Luke 4:18).

Through his own eyes, man cannot see beyond his lack. He can only see that there is always more to be done and more to be grasped for, so he grasps in his own strength. From the beginning it has been the lies of the enemy that have blinded man to the true generosity of God and caused him to grasp for independence from God (Genesis 3:1–6, 2 Corinthians 4:4). Sin is the fruit of this root lie, for whatever man thinks or does that is not rooted in faith in God is sin (Romans 14:23).

In contrast to man-made religion's demands on us to do enough, God's Holy Spirit opens our eyes to see that what Jesus accomplished for us is already enough, in fact more than enough, to reconcile us to God totally and provide for all of our needs (Romans 5:17, Matthew 7:11). Through God's eyes, man can see that everything that needs to be done has already been done for him by Christ (1 Corinthians 2:12). There is no middle ground or balance between religion and the gospel of Christ's finished work. Religion says "do;" the gospel says "done!"

The gospel declares to us all, both believers and non-believers: "stop trying to make yourself right with God!" What God wants to do in and through our lives is to demonstrate His righteousness and His life. The light of the world is His righteousness and His love, not ours. Our families don't need to see our righteousness. This nation is fed up with self-righteousness and man-made religion which drives people away. Let them see Jesus in us. Let them see Jesus in the church. Let them see *His* righteousness and *His* love in us. But before they can see it, we have to see it first!

We, as the church, have to, as Paul instructed the Colossians, remember how we first received Christ (as a gift) and continue to walk with God on the basis that all good things that come from Him can only be received as a gift. This truth causes our lives to overflow continually in thankfulness (Colossians 2:6–7).

If we dilute this truth, we dilute the joy of our salvation and the strength of the church. The extent to which the gospel of Christ's righteousness has been subtly replaced by a gospel about our righteousness can be seen in the lack of joy in Christ's church and the widespread perception of unbelievers that the Christian life is not primarily one of joy, but one of hard work and rule-keeping. To walk through this life accepting God's blessings as a gift, rather than a reward, requires humility. If we begin to believe that our record and our religious performance are what "releases" the blessings of God, then we will estrange and distance ourselves from Christ and His abundant life, for His life was first given to us as a gift and will always remain a gift, for salvation is of the Lord (Psalm 37:39, Jonah 2:9, Romans 8:3).

It is a humbling experience to come to the place of knowing that there is nothing we can add to the finished work of Jesus on the cross, and to all who will remain in that place of dependency, grace flows (James 4:6). Don't make your life about how much you love

God. Make it about how much He loves you (1 John 4:10). Peter boasted in his love for Jesus, but John spoke of Jesus's love for him. Only one of them was left standing at the cross. If you are desperate to do something for God, then why not do the one thing He asks us to do: believe in Christ! (John 6:28–29) Believe in His life and His obedience, and not in your own! (Romans 5:19)

It is a great truth that there is nothing we can do in the flesh to add to Christ's finished work, which is the foundation for worshiping God in spirit and in truth. We cannot truly worship Him in the spirit unless all confidence in flesh has gone (Philippians 3:3).

John began His Gospel by describing Jesus as "full of grace and truth" and then immediately declared in John 1:16 an extraordinary statement: "And of his fullness have all we received, and grace for grace." This message of the completeness of Christ's work in us—the message of His fullness in us—is the message that was proclaimed in the early church and it is the truth that emboldened them to *be* Christ in their generation, rather than a pale imitation of Christ. Jesus did not suffer for the sins of the world and die on the cross so that we could merely try and imitate Him in gratitude. He died, not that we might live for Him with all *our* strength, but that He would live in us in all *His* strength, for only by *His* Spirit can we live in the fullness of *His* life (Philippians 2:13). Our strength and best efforts to imitate Him only get in the way and distance us from the grace that enables *His* life to dwell in us (Galatians 5:2). That is why Paul said that he found the strength of God in him at times of his greatest weakness or need (2 Corinthians 1:8–9), for at times when we can no longer see a way forward in the natural realm, we can only see our way forward by seeing in the Spirit, and only the Spirit can show man that in Christ we have already risen and overcome this world (1 Corinthians 2:14, Ephesians 2:6, Colossians 3:1–3, 2 Corinthians 5:16).

He died so that we, like Him, could be full of grace and truth, not just in the next life but in *this* life, too! (1 John 4:17, Colossians 3:4) Listen to the apostle John proclaim again the completeness of Christ's work in every believer recorded in 1 John 4:17: "Herein is our love made perfect, that we may have boldness in the day of judgment: because as he is, so are we in this world."[36]

Why does John declare such extraordinary things about us? Because he and the early church discovered a very simple truth in those amazing days: extraordinary lives are lived by people who believe extraordinary things! Is the good news that God has found a way to make His home in men not the most extraordinary thing in the world to believe? Believing anything less would be a lesser life; an ordinary religious life of mere men. But Christian, do you not know who you are now because of what Christ has done? Is the Holy Spirit not still effectively saying to us as the church, "Why do you still live as mere men, separated from God, when in God's reality you now are the temple of the living God, his very home?" (1 Corinthians 3:3, 16)

As believers, we cannot start to manifest the fullness of the Christ life until we start to believe that the Christ life is in us, and that we are now the temple of the living God (1 Corinthians 6:17). In other words, we will not live out the life that God has already freely given us—His full and complete life—until we start to see ourselves as He sees us: full of His life and complete in Him (Colossians 2:10).

It may come as a shock to some of us that the primary work of the Holy Spirit in believers is not to convince us we are imperfect. The Spirit does not need to reveal to us what we can see in the natural realm. He comes to reveal to us what we need to see in the Spirit and what God sees: the perfection and completeness of His work in us (1 Corinthians 2:14). That completeness refers to our spirit, not our

---

[36] King James Version.

bodies or our souls (Ephesians 1:13). But in this world, to live in the completeness and fullness of Christ's life and Spirit in us, we have to learn to live out of who we are in our spirits, not who we are in our souls (Ephesians 4:21–24). If you believe that at the core of your very being is merely a natural man that the world sees and relates to; then you will live that out (Proverbs 23:7). You will live out of your soul, the realm of your emotions, and your intellect. You will live merely by the information your five natural senses give you (1 Corinthians 2:14). You will live as the person you *feel* yourself to be. Multitudes of spiritually immature Christians live like this for years and our self-centered, anxious, competitive lives do little to reveal the victory or union of Christ with His church (1 Corinthians 3:3). If everything is going well in our lives this week and all of our prayers appear to be being answered, then we *feel* ourselves to be Christians. But if next week, everything in our lives has gone wrong and none of our prayers appear to be answered, then suddenly we don't *feel* like Christians. Living in the soulish realm, where how we feel is how we live, is like living like a wave tossed to and fro by every wind of circumstance (James 1:6). This is where many of us have lived for years, because we have not been properly established in the truth of our reconciliation with God and our union with Christ (2 Corinthians 5:18–21). We have not been rooted and established in love and therefore cannot grasp that the trials that we face are not an indicator of God turning His back on us (Ephesians 3:17–19). How can He turn His back on the one He has made His very back and His very body? (Romans 8:31–39, Ephesians 5:29) Yet if we remain living out of our souls rather than our spirits, from our feelings rather than faith, living from the natural rather than the spiritual realm, then the claims of the gospel of our union with Christ sound foolish to us (1 Corinthians 2:14). When someone declares to us that God has already given us everything we need and that He has already blessed us with every spiritual blessing in the heavenly realms in Christ Jesus, we struggle to believe it, because that is not how we feel. As believers who have lived for so long in the soulish realm of our feelings, we have come to the conclusion that who we are is who we feel ourselves to be! The gospel calls us to rise out of this soulish natural realm and start to set our minds on things above and our vision on the heavenly realms and the truth of our position in Christ, which is high and lifted up, seated together with God (Colossians 3:2). This is the purpose of the gospel, for the full proclamation of the gospel is not just the news that Christ died for us, but that we died and our life is now hidden with Christ in God (Colossians 3:3). This is not to say that it is wrong for us to be emotional or to have strong feelings, but simply that our emotions should not be directed by fear, but informed and led by a mind renewed by the Spirit (Ephesians 4:23–24). We have been made body, soul, and spirit by God. The Christian gospel is good news for all of us! God is Spirit but He "became" flesh. He did not despise our bodies and neither should we. In fact the scriptures compare Christ's love for His church to the way we each nourish and cherish our own bodies (Ephesians 5:29). Christ, our head, has united Himself with each believer and each believer is a body, soul, and spirit being. Can any greater compliment be paid to our bodies than to be declared "the temple of the Holy Spirit?" (1 Corinthians 6:19) Yet as believers, we do not live from the mere natural requirements or desires of our bodies, nor the fears of our souls. We are not to be ruled by our natural senses or our natural intellect. Neither our stomachs nor our brains are to be our gods (Philippians 3:19), rather setting our minds on Christ allows us to live from the mind of the Spirit, our identity, and our personality, rooted and established in our union with Christ. Such a life, established in grace, flows from the Spirit through our souls and bodies into the natural realm like a river of life (John 7:38).

This truth of our reconciliation to God and the new life of union He freely provides is not just about an intellectual assent, but is communicated to us as a living reality by the presence of the Holy Spirit in us. Some people look to gain access to a country by marrying a citizen of that country. Their citizenship is purchased by that marriage certificate, but she is not a real bride. These are known as "sham marriages." Many believers live as if their union with Christ is a sham marriage. They believe in the legality of the transaction and they claim the benefits of heavenly citizenship, but they do not live in the reality of an active union with the same Spirit that rose Christ from the dead. A believer who continues to be a slave to his natural fears and appetites may have his citizenship in heaven, but His mind has not yet been renewed to think from there and therefore to live from there. God's purpose in giving us the gift and the baptism of His Holy Spirit was that there would not just be a reception or a flowing in to his innermost being of the life of God, but an outpouring and a flowing from. Wherever the river of life flows, it brings forth great fruit in the land through which it flows (Ezekiel 47:12, Revelation 22:2). By the grace of God, as we learn to let the truth of God flow from us to others, the land through which those living waters flow—our souls and our bodies—cannot help but be blessed (Proverbs 4:20–22). So let the river flow! Let us live from and speak from the realities that all heaven knows: the sufficiency and the supremacy of Christ's work to provide for our every need in life. Let us refuse to live from the mere appearance of things to the natural senses, for if all believers did that, how would the voice of God be heard on the earth?

Jesus said, "God is Spirit and those who worship Him *must* worship in Spirit and in truth" (John 4:23, emphasis added). If our eyes do not open to see by the Spirit, and if we do not wake up to who we are now in God's eyes, then so many scriptures, such as 2 Corinthians 5:17, make no sense. "Therefore, if anyone is in Christ, he is a new creation; old things have passed away; behold, all things have become new." The Holy Spirit leads us into the wonderful truth of the enormity of what Christ has done for us. He enables us to see what we have not seen before: the fullness of God's kindness to us in the face of Christ (2 Corinthians 4:6) and in seeing Him, what we believe and our very lives (Proverbs 4:23) are transformed from glory to glory, for by the Spirit, believing is seeing! (2 Corinthians 3:18)

Chapter 11

Living from the finished work of Christ

"I have glorified thee on the earth. I have finished the work which you gave me to do."

John 17:4

"Therefore, if anyone is in Christ, he is a new creation; old things have passed away; behold, all things have become new."

2 Corinthians 5:17

Notice how the second verse above is at odds with our feelings. If we live by our feelings, then on many days we don't feel like old things have passed away. We don't feel like all things have become new. We feel that one day, in the sweet by and by, we will become that new creation that God had in mind, but not today, because we see ourselves only through our old soulish mind, a mind conformed to the natural world and not yet renewed by the truth (Romans 12:2). But God's Word does not say that one day you will be a new creation, for that is an ordinary thing to say and God's Word never says anything ordinary about us (John 7:46). It says the extraordinary over us so that we would live the extraordinary life: the Christ life. God's Word declares that if anyone is in Christ He *is* a new creation.

It has been to the great detriment of the church that this aspect of the finished work of Christ—the union of Christ with the believer—has been neglected. Rather than setting our minds on things above, where we have been seated with Christ and begin to live from (Ephesians 2:6), we remain as the disciples did on the day of Christ's ascension; peering at the sky, wondering when Jesus will come to us again. We have proclaimed the truth about *His* resurrection and *His* ascension, but our silence on the subject of *our* ascension reveals how much of the modern church's vision and life remains tied to the natural realm. Hence the strength of the church is measured by natural means (numbers, finances, political influence). A conference on "church growth" will usually mean learning new techniques to attract more or retain members. They rarely refer to the growth of the church out of the natural realm into the spiritual. Natural thinking can accept the concept that Jesus died *for* us, but only by the Spirit can the church see that Jesus died *as* us; that when He died, so did we, that when He rose, so did we, and that when He ascended and sat down in the place of rest and victory, so did we (Ephesians 2:6). To the natural man, it may appear that a believer's or a church's busyness, their programs and various works, are the measure of their spiritual maturity, or perhaps even their abstinence or separation from the affairs of the world. But both of these can be done with no revelation of the victory already achieved. Some of the largest and busiest churches in Christendom are full of deeply anxious believers who live in a constant state of sin-consciousness due to sitting under teaching that mixes the Old with the New Covenant. That "little leaven" of religious teaching causes their gaze to drop from Christ and onto themselves, just enough to keep their vision and their thinking largely in the natural realm. Even though they may operate with the gifts of the Spirit, their vision remains that of disciples who feel that Christ is separate from them. They constantly remain more conscious of their soulish inadequacies than their spiritual completeness and this is continually reflected in their teaching and subject matter. Christians, i.e. people of the New Covenant, who regularly sit under a mixed message of the gospel and the Law, grace and religion, never mature properly into walking by the Spirit (Galatians 3:25). It is hard for a bird to fly in the heavens when one wing is chained to the earth. Christians who put their faith in the schoolmaster of the Law to keep them from sin deprive themselves of a far superior victory over sin in this life: walking in the Spirit. To the Galatians, who had been wrongly pointed toward the Old Covenant as an aid to their faith, Paul declared this: "So I say, walk by the Spirit, and you will not gratify the desires of the flesh. For the flesh desires what is contrary to the Spirit, and the Spirit what is contrary to the flesh. They are in conflict with each other, so that you are not to do whatever you want. But if you are led by the Spirit, you are not under the law"[37] (Galatians 5:16–18). Despite the clear warning by scripture that the Law is powerless to change us (Romans 8:3, Hebrews 7:19, 10:1), that only the covenant of grace frees us from the dominion of sin (Romans 6:14), that the Law gives sin its power (1 Corinthians 15:56), and that the Law was only our guardian *until* Christ (Galatians 3:24[38]), most believers across the body of Christ are still reared from Sunday School on a mixed message of the Law and grace. This mixture (normally justified by the term "balanced") still produces classical Galatians; powerless Christians (Galatians 5:4). To these anxious souls, a busy church program is an opportunity to keep sin and guilt at a manageable level and persuade God to bless them. This is not the victorious abundant life of which Jesus spoke.

To walk in the Spirit is to see what God sees. A believer who cannot see that all the promises of God are now "Yes" and not "Maybe" or "perhaps depending on…" is a believer that cannot see that they are now *in* Christ, "For all of God's promises have been fulfilled in Christ with a resounding 'Yes!' And through Christ,

---

[37] New International Version.
[38] Young's Literal Translation.

our 'Amen' (which means 'Yes') ascends to God for his glory"[39] (2 Corinthians 1:20).

What glorifies God is a church that humbly accepts the gift of the ascended, victorious life of union with God and thereby gives all the glory to God for salvation. This allows His grace to flow in our lives to the measure that He desires, an abundant measure that reveals the supernatural love, character, and glory of our God to this world (Ephesians 3:8–11). The Holy Spirit does not drive the sheep; He leads them (John 10:27). He does not need to use guilt or fear to drive us in the right direction, for He pours into our hearts the love of God and His love matures and perfects us so that His walk becomes ours (Luke 24:32).

If you will not believe that through Christ, God has already given you His righteousness, then you will grasp for righteousness, and just as Eve reached for the fruit that looked good, you will reach out toward religion and eat, thinking that holiness is something you can attain through what you do. But in eating of that system (doing to become) you will be like Snow White eating the poisoned apple. Your eyes will close to the reality of the world of the Spirit, the world where sin has been dealt with and Christ has sat down and us with Him. You will find yourself asleep to that reality and living instead in a bad dream, where Christ's work on the cross has changed nothing and holiness and righteousness is something that you do not yet have, but must work for by the sweat of your brow. Such work is evil in God's eyes because it is anti-Christ; it denies the finished work of Christ. The Greek word that is translated as "evil" 71 times in the New Testament is the word *poneros*. This is Strong's definition of this word: "full of labours, annoyances, hardships pressed and harassed by labours bringing toils." (Strong's G4190)

---

[39] New Living Translation.

Imagine a man who has been told he can earn a great prize by running a marathon. At what point would he be more likely to humble himself and accept the prize as a gift rather than a reward? If he believes that all his labor and toil have brought him near the finish line and that he has managed in his own strength nearly to complete the 26 miles, he will really struggle to accept the prize as a gift. But if he knows that all his best efforts have not even got him off the starting block, then He will gladly and joyfully receive the prize (holiness and righteousness) as a gift.

Why do so many Christians struggle to receive righteousness and favor with God as a gift? Why do we resist the revelation that in Christ, we have already received all that we will ever need to live the shared life He has called us to? (Ephesians 2:4–7) Why do we think that the blessings of God, including healing, are dependent on how well we are doing church or doing life?

Could it be because, like the elder brother, years of struggle and effort to please God have nurtured a belief, hidden in our hearts, that all of our suffering must have managed by now to get us closer to His blessing? So to hear of the Father's blessing of grace, freely given to great sinners, strikes us as irrational and unjust (Luke 15:28–32, Matthew 21:31–32). What about all the sacrifices we have made as Christians down through the years, where is our reward? (Luke 15:29–30) The only answer to such hurt is to receive revelation from the Holy Spirit that in fact all our best efforts to earn the prize of union with God never even got us off the starting block. We have a Father who, knowing this, never asked us to earn His eternal life, but shared all He had with us right at the beginning of our journey (Romans 5:8, Luke 15:12). The prize of this Christian race we are running was never eternal life (that was obtained for us), but knowing Him more and more (Philippians 3:7–14), and through knowing Him finding ourselves to be like Him (1 John 3:2). What a discovery that to all who receive Him as He really is—gracious enough to freely give—they can know what it is to live by His grace as "children of God" (John 1:12), able to live from righteousness, peace, and joy from the glorious Kingdom (Romans 14:17).

In the city of Philippi, Paul and Silas were whipped and then chained up in a dungeon for preaching the gospel (Acts 16:23–26). That night it was obvious to them and to the other prisoners that in the natural realm, all hope that could be seen was gone (Acts 16:16–40). But what was their response? It doesn't say that Paul and Silas cried out to Jesus to get up from His seat in heaven and do something to bring them victory. Instead, they started to sing a song of victory and praise and the atmosphere and the power of heaven prevailed and broke into the natural realm. An earthquake shook the very foundations of that prison and all of their chains fell off (Acts 16:25–26). Remarkable as that was, was it not more remarkable that Paul and Silas had been singing as if their chains were already broken? By living by the revelation of the Spirit, they saw what the Spirit saw. They did not sing in order to reach victory, rather they sang *from* victory. They didn't demand that God line up His actions to their reality, rather they lined up their actions to God's reality; that in prison, they were no less loved or provided for in Christ than if they had been in a palace! (John 19:10–11) That's the difference between disciples of Jesus *before* Pentecost (when the Holy Spirit came) and *after*. Before the coming of the Spirit, when the disciples found themselves in a storm, they saw their only hope as getting Jesus to do something. In the boat in the storm, they looked to get Jesus woken up and on His feet (Mark 4:38). When mobbed by thousands of hungry people in the wilderness, they went looking for Jesus to do something (Matthew 14:15). When Jesus said that He was leaving them, Peter protested, as he could not imagine how they could ever do what Jesus did (Matthew 16:22).

But *after* the Holy Spirit came, when the disciples found themselves in trouble, they didn't cry out to Jesus to do something; they instead declared what Jesus had done. No longer did they bring sick people to Jesus to see what He would say; they spoke directly to the sickness themselves (Acts 3:6). No longer did they talk about taking over the government of the day so they could influence men and change things, they just started to govern the natural realm through the power of the Spirit (Acts 14:8–18). No longer did they point people to the sky and say, "One day the kingdom of God will come." They preached the gospel and declared that the King had already come and set up His throne and dominion in their lives, enabling them to do what Jesus said they would do; heal the sick and declare, "The kingdom of God has come near to you"[40] (Luke 10:9). Isn't it amazing? Apparently we don't need a sound system, lights, and a crowd for the world to see "revival." They just need to see people who look like they have nothing, but live like they have everything! (1 Corinthians 3:21–23)

This same Holy Spirit has been given to us so that we can see what those disciples could see…just how much has already been freely given to us! (1 Corinthians 2:12) If we do not see by the Spirit what is already ours—that in Christ, victory is already ours—then we will spend our lives crying out for Jesus to do something and then getting upset with Him that He doesn't appear to have done anything.

I wonder how many Christians have been slowly and quietly crushed in their spirits, waiting in vain for God to do something He has already done (Proverbs 13:12). Without the revelation that He has never withheld from us what we have been asking Him for, believers can easily build up anger within themselves (Luke 15:28–32). Unlike the elder brother, who directed his anger at the Father, many Christians either direct it at those around them, criticizing and dividing, or unhealthily suppress anger, which can lead to depression and other signs of a "crushed spirit" (Proverbs 17:22).

---

[40] New International Version.

Why is it so important that the church speak up of the enormity of what Christ has done and tell the world that in Him all the promises of God, the God "who forgives ALL your sins and heals ALL your diseases"[41] (Psalm 103:3), are "Yes" in Christ? (2 Corinthians 1:20) Why should we keep telling people that in Christ they have already been forgiven and healed (Hebrews 10:14, 1 Peter 2:24), even though often all they have ever known is guilt and sickness? Because doing anything else would take people's hope off Christ and subtly move it back onto themselves. The moment you believe that there is something you need to do to prompt God to act on your behalf (pray more, give more, get more faith, live holier), *before* He will forgive you or heal you, you have just returned to the Old Covenant, to being "under the Law," for now your hope is back on the strength of your flesh and your performance. You have placed yourself as living before the cross, waiting for a Savior to come. Paul and Silas did not start to sing in that dungeon so that God would come. They sang because they were living from the revelation that He had already come!

So to all who come to the church for answers, to those who sit in dungeons of depression, sickness and grief, chained to their past, we dare to sing over them and speak over them of their victory in Christ. We dare to speak of things that are not as if they are (Romans 4:17), for on hearing this glorious news of what He has already accomplished, faith comes, and through faith in Christ (not faith in our faith), men are born from above and can begin to live from above. Whether that earthquake ever came or not, whether their prison doors flew open or not, Paul and Silas would not have stopped singing, for they were already free. We also choose to preach and sing of victory, even in the face of no outward change in a situation, because our song has never been about what God may do if we sing well enough, but of what He has already done. Paul and Silas did

---

[41] New International Version.

not need those doors to fly open in order to believe, for the gospel had already set them free to live in joy in all seasons. This is why we preach the gospel of Christ's finished work, not so that God would come down, but so that men would rise up to live from the exalted position He died to place them in; to be in Christ (Ephesians 2:4–9). We preach the gospel not just to the world, but to the church, so that she would leave the field of religion and enter into the joy of the Father. Her entering in causes the sound of music and dancing—the sound of victory—to spread out across the world, as the knowledge that heaven already has begins to cover the earth; that through the gift of Christ, the Father has withheld no good thing from man. The abolition of religion has been declared, God has reconciled the world to Himself, and the Holy Spirit has gone out into the fields of religion with a message to the church: "Set down your tools. Your labor at what has already been finished only estranges you from the joy of your Father. Through Christ, religion has been abolished. Everything He has now belongs to you and there is only one fitting response. You must begin to celebrate, for what was dead has been brought back to life, what was lost has been found. To the enemy, your laughter is the revelation of his defeat (1 Samuel 14:15–16) and to your Father in heaven, it is the prize He gave everything to secure" (Luke 15:31–32).

Chapter 12

Prosperity is Christ

> "So we have stopped evaluating others from a human point of view. At one time we thought of Christ merely from a human point of view. How differently we know him now!"[42]
>
> 2 Corinthians 5:16

Thinking from a merely human point of view will restrict us from seeing as God sees (1 Samuel 16:7, Isaiah 55:9). Only the Holy Spirit changes our thinking so that we may begin to perceive and know how God thinks and sees. No human mind could ever comprehend the thoughts of God, but here is the staggering truth about everyone who receives God's Holy Spirit: our minds are no longer merely human, for we now have the mind of Christ (1 Corinthians 2:16). Even this concept is foolishness to the natural mind without the Holy Spirit to enlighten us as to just how much has been freely given to us through Christ (1 Corinthians 2:12). We have been given the Holy Spirit that we may now rise in our thoughts to think from God's point of view (Isaiah 55:8–9). He seated us in the heavenly realms so that our perspective on life would be totally different; so that we may see as God sees. But what does it mean to see as God sees?

---

[42] New Living Translation.

To see as God sees is about seeing men in light of what God has done, not just in light of what they have done (Acts 10:15). To see as God sees is about seeing that Christ's life, death, and resurrection radically changed how God relates to men and therefore how we should relate to him (Acts 10:28). Christ completely fulfilled the Law and, in His body, took the judgment for the sins of the whole world (John 1:29, 1 John 2:2). This change is so radical that for people who have been brought up focusing on sin management and how to keep it at a respectable level, we usually take some time to be weaned off defining righteousness before God as *our* obedience and onto Christ's obedience (Romans 5:19). If we have spent a lifetime thinking in Old Covenant terms of people being either "clean" or "unclean" to a holy God, then we may find ourselves naturally resistant to the full implications of the gospel, that the way is now open for *all* men to approach God and receive His grace, His Spirit, and His eternal life through faith in Christ (1 John 2:2). Certainly the early church, being Jewish and steeped in the culture of the Law, remained resistant for some time to the new reality of the New Covenant (Acts 10:14). The new reality was that there was no longer a separation between Jews and Gentiles, in the sense that human parentage or performance no longer qualified a person to enjoy God's covenant blessing (Galatians 3:28, Colossians 3:11). Instead, just as under God's covenant with Abraham, men would be counted righteous by faith and by believing Christ to be the true revelation of God (Romans 4:3). It was hard for those early Jewish Christians, who had always thought of Jews alone as God's covenant people, to accept that God wanted Gentiles (non-Jews) to know his blessings also. Yet this is exactly what Jesus had been pointing to throughout His ministry (Matthew 21:33–46, 22:1–14). The apostle Paul had been commissioned for this very purpose; to go to the Gentiles with the gospel of God's New Covenant (Acts 9:15). He believed that God had always intended to extend the covenant of grace that God had made with Abraham to all men (Galatians 3:14). He believed that, now that the covenant of the Law had been fulfilled by Christ and was no longer in operation, God's blessing was no longer tied to a person's parentage or performance in the natural realm (Romans 10:4, Hebrews 10:9). It was this truth that he emphasized to the Galatians, as he warned them of the futility of seeking to justify themselves before God through their religion. This is summed up in Galatians 3:11–14.

> "Now that no one is justified by the Law before God is evident; for, 'The righteous man shall live by faith.' However, the Law is not of faith; on the contrary, 'He who practices them shall live by them.' Christ redeemed us from the curse of the Law, having become a curse for us—for it is written, 'Cursed is everyone who hangs on a tree'—in order that in Christ Jesus the blessing of Abraham might come to the Gentiles, so that we would receive the promise of the Spirit through faith."[43]

Not having been raised Jewish, it is hard for us to grasp the difficulty that those raised in an Old Covenant culture had in transitioning from thinking exclusively (the blessing of Abraham is only for his physical descendants) to thinking inclusively (the blessing of Abraham is for all who will believe). Despite the outpouring of the Holy Spirit, for several years, apostles like Peter still did not understand that God wanted them to bring the gospel to the whole world, not just the Jews (Acts 10:14, Galatians 2:11–12). They were still looking at men from a natural or human point of view, not seeing from God's perspective that the work of Christ (the last Adam) was just as comprehensive as the work of the first Adam (1 Corinthians 15:20–22, 45). They understood from their history and prophets that God dealt with the nation of Israel according to its performance. They failed to see that, under the New Covenant

---

[43] New American Standard Bible.

that Jesus had brought in, God was no longer prepared to limit His blessing to men because of their human parentage or performance (Acts 10:28). To enable Him to freely give to man as much blessing as He wanted, God had to make a covenant with a man who would perfectly reciprocate His love and devotion, thus fulfilling all the requirements of the Law (Matthew 22:37–40). Only a God man could do this, so God became flesh and dwelt among men (John 1:14). God's new covenant is with Himself, for the Father and the Son are one, and now any man can benefit from this covenant, not by his human parentage or performance, but by his position "in Christ." This privilege is freely extended to all men by grace, for it is the will of God that no man should perish (2 Peter 3:9) But this gift can only be received by faith (Ephesians 2:8). Men must believe and God gives man every aid to help Him (John 1:4), yet perfect love must allow freedom of choice. No one can be forced by God to love Him or receive Him. No matter how much God desires that we receive His love and sweet fellowship, love will never force us, only woo us (1 Corinthians 13:4–7). Men may refuse the love of God and so remain separate from Him forever (John 3:20, 2 Thessalonians 1:9). This has always broken the heart of God, for the love of God encompasses His enemies as well as His friends (Luke 13:34, 23:34).

Scholars may differ as to what "hell"—eternal separation from God—means, but scripture is clear that hell exists (Mark 9:43) and that God doesn't want anyone to go there or else He would not have died for the sins of the whole world (John 1:29, 1 John 2:2). All men who refuse God's free gift of life through Christ stand condemned to receive what they have desired: separation from God (John 3:18).

In Jesus's story of the prodigal son, the Father represents God and it is important that we see that, throughout that story, the Father never imposes His will on either of His two sons (Luke 15:12, 28). He has made a way for all who desire Him to be with Him, for He has taken away the sins of the whole world (John 1:29, 1 John 2:2). He has reconciled the whole world to Himself and now invites all men to be reconciled—to be who He sees them to be—by believing the gospel (2 Corinthians 5:19-21). God is so willing that no one should perish that He even supplies the very faith to believe (Romans 10:17). That power is in the gospel itself, for the good news is so powerful that it doesn't have to demand faith of men, for the power to believe comes with the gospel message (Romans 1:16). The only qualification to receive Christ is that you want Him (John 4:10, John 7:37).

As Jesus described the Father going out to implore the elder brother to join Him, He already carried in His heart that same grief of seeing many reject and resist being gathered to the Father (Matthew 23:37). When we see Jesus weep over those who chose darkness instead of light (John 3:19) and rejected Him, we understand that God sent light into the world because his will is that no one remain in darkness (John 1:9). It is not possible to see this world as God sees it without being filled with the love He has for a world that rejects Him; a love that refuses to take away man's free will (Luke 23:34). This is why the Holy Spirit is given to us; so that we would experience the unconditional love of God for this world and therefore see this world through His loving eyes (Romans 5:5).

Knowing the truth that in Christ we lack no good thing deals with the lie planted in mankind, whose fruit was sin (Genesis 3:1). The devil planted a seed in mankind; a lie that, when received and believed, produced a harvest called sin, which produced death (James 1:15). The lie told to man in the garden was in effect this: God has not shared His full life with you, but you can get that life by grasping for it. That lie of lack caused Adam and Eve to start to live as if they did not have a share in God's life, as if God had not breathed His life in them and given them His image and likeness. When you believe that you lack something, you will look to grasp for it, and that is the root of all sin. That's why the Bible says that "the love of money is the root of all kinds of evil" (1

Timothy 6:10), because the desire for money is a manifestation of the lie that I do not have enough, the lie that God has not shared His abundant life with me. God does not have a problem with us being wealthy, but He does have an issue with us chasing wealth, for if we are trying to grasp something, it reveals that we don't believe we already have it.

The provision of God is already there for every believer to do what God has called us to do—to be like our Father in heaven—for His life is already in us (2 Peter 1:3). That life—His life—is a complete life (Colossians 2:10). He is not lacking in any area, whether it be the area of righteousness, health, or provision. Now when we believe that, a remarkable thing happens; we stop striving to do all the things we think we need to do to grasp the provision of God (1 Corinthians 3:21–23). We discover that believing that we already have all that we need in Christ causes a contentment to rise in us, so that we are content in every season of life. Irrespective of the appearance of things, the witness of the Holy Spirit in us is that we will have what we need in the hour that we need it (John 11:6–7). He teaches us to focus on hearing the will of the Father (John 10:27), not striving to find new ways to get Him to hear our will!

Many Christians work on their confession and on their sowing and reaping because they believe that it will bring them great gain and that great gain will be a sign of their godliness and will in turn bring them contentment. But the Bible does not say that great gain will bring you contentment. It says that contentment with godliness *is* great gain.

My father once told me that when the richest man in the world was asked how much more money he would need to be content, his reply was, "Just a little more." If we won't believe the truth that we already have in Christ everything we need to live the Christ life, then no amount of money will make us content (Ecclesiastes 3:11). The heart was designed to be satisfied, content, and at rest only in the truth, and the truth is that we have no call to chase after wealth and pierce ourselves through with many sorrows, for God has not withheld the fullness and completeness of His life from us (1 Timothy 6:10). All the teaching I have on finance can be summed up in one verse: "He who did not spare his own Son, but gave him up for us all—how will he not also, along with him, graciously give us all things?"[44] (Romans 8:32)

What does the life of Christ teach us about finances? In the hour when Jesus needed enough resources to do what He had been called to do, whether that was to feed five thousand or seven thousand people, He always found that He had more than enough (Mark 8:19–20). His need for provision was always met, not because of what He did, but because of who He was—the son of a generous Father. When questioned about the miracles in His life, Jesus's explanation was not that He managed to persuade His Father to fund His life, but rather that He only ever walked into what the Father asked of Him (John 5:19). The key to knowing the bountiful provision of God in our lives is knowing His will, for He provides for that which He ordains (Ephesians 2:10). No matter how many confessions of faith we make, or how many financial seeds we sow, God will not provide for something that is simply outside His will for our lives. He wants us to know His will for our lives and gives us His Holy Spirit and His Word so that our minds would be renewed to His will (Romans 12:2). Giving people the impression that God can be cajoled into releasing provision (such as finance or healing) into our lives if we just hit on the right method or confession, not only demeans the character of Him who gave everything to us when we deserved nothing (Romans 5:8), but also sets people up to become disappointed or angry with God when their demands are not supplied.

---

[44] New International Version.

In the hour that we need the finance to do the work we are called to—living the Christ life—we will have what we need, not because of what we do, but because of who we are through what Christ has done; children of a generous father (Matthew 4:4). Some teach various principles or laws of what we need to *do* to get the provision of God into our lives. It is true that wise stewardship of our resources will benefit us, but the emphasis of these teachings is invariably on our faithfulness, diligence, obedience, or confession. The danger is that, slowly but surely, our hope moves from the sure ground of what God has done through Christ's obedience and onto the sands of what God may do through our obedience.

The more we see the generosity of the Father, the more we become like Him (2 Corinthians 3:18). The more we believe what the Holy Spirit is revealing to us about how blessed we already are in Christ, the more the generosity of the Father overflows through our giving (Galatians 5:16), for perfect love casts out fear.

Of course Christians should give generously to others, but if that giving is to glorify God, it must be of the Spirit, not of the flesh. It must be born out of the revelation of who we already are: co-heirs with Christ (Romans 8:17), lacking nothing (Psalm 34:10), rather than born out of our doubts and insecurities about whether we have given enough to impress God. Here is the gospel that sets men free: Christ impressed God on our behalf! We have a plentiful supply of all we need through Christ's obedience and His sowing, for He sowed all that was necessary for us to reap the life of God (John 12:24, 10:18).

This revelation of our identity in Christ as sons of a generous Father frees us from self and empowers us to pour out our lives for others as Jesus did, in the power of the generous Spirit (John 5:30). We can give as Jesus gave; because He wanted to, not because He was working a principle for a return! (Matthew 23:23–24) This is why the manifestation of true prosperity in our lives is not seen by what we gather to ourselves, but rather what we give away to others (Luke 21:1–4). So prosperity in the life of a believer manifests as a pouring out of our lives for others. But the source of that pouring out is not a sense of lack (if I sow this, then God will have to bless me), but rather a revelation that I lose nothing by pouring out because God has eternally given all things into my hands (John 13:3–5). If we do not give in the revelation that all things in Christ are ours (giving in the Spirit), then we have not given freely for we have been obliged to give by our fear of lack. Without a revelation that through Christ, God has freely given to us all that He has, then we cannot give freely. As Jesus sent His twelve disciples off to represent Him, He instructed them on how to truly represent Him with these words, "Freely you have received, freely give" (Matthew 10:8).

God wants us to give freely, for our liberty from fear glorifies Him and reveals His love to be perfect and perfecting (1 John 4:18). Confident, free children are a great testimony to their parents. It is for such freedom that we have been set free (Galatians 5:1). We were not set free to work at principles to earn God's blessing. As a believer, if you want to work at your sowing and reaping, by all means keep working. Your Father still loves you and you still have eternal life, it's just that you have put off enjoying the fullness of that life. Without a revelation that in Christ, they already have all they need, multitudes of Christians live with their hope as "God will bless me one day," rather than "Christ is in me *today!*" (Colossians 1:27) The elder brother in Jesus's parable of the prodigal son spoke from a heart sickened by disappointment that his day to be blessed had not yet come. The response of the Father is still the revelation the Holy Spirit would speak to a church waiting for what has already been given: "Son, you are always with me, and all that I have is yours" (Luke 15:31).

The teachings of Christ reveal to us that God provides for us like a Father does for His children, not merely as an employer to His workers. In Jesus's parable of the prodigal son, it was the elder brother's insistence that the Father relate to him on the basis of what he had done, not who he was, that prevented the elder son from entering into the Father's joy (Luke 15:28). Christians can relate to the Father on the basis of sowing and reaping and have needs met, but there is a realm of joy and liberty from which we exclude ourselves if we insist on shackling God's generosity to our performance.

Indeed, a man reaps what he sows, but isn't it the same for God? What seed has He sown into the life of every believer? (Luke 8:11) Is it not the very life of Christ in us to which the Father now relates? (John 4:24) Whose obedience is it that has released to us the abundant overflowing life of God; ours or Christ's?

It was the obedience of one that brought us out of works and into rest (Romans 5:19). Having begun His life in us in this way; by giving us everything and by withholding no good thing from us (Romans 8:32), why would God now change his mind and ask that we complete the good work that He began; the supplying of abundant life? (Galatians 3:3, Colossians 2:6) Do you really think that after a few hours of that celebration of the prodigal son's return, the Father would have turned around and said to him: "That's the end of the honeymoon. Now get yourself over to the servant's quarters, find some tools and get busy if you want my generosity to continue. From now on I only bless you according to your sowing!"

How could this be the same Father that gave that son everything he had, when the son had done nothing to earn it? (Luke 15:12, Romans 5:8) If Jesus is the same yesterday, today, and forever, then so is the Father (Hebrews 13:8). If God gave you the best He had to give when you had done nothing to deserve it, what makes you think that He has changed His mind and now gives to you on the basis of what your sowing deserves? To those concerned about having enough, Jesus did not point to men working in the field to plant seed and say "Look at how they sow for that is the way to ensure you always have enough." Instead He pointed to the birds of the air and declared "Look at the birds of the air, that they do not sow, nor reap nor gather into barns, and yet your heavenly Father feeds them. Are you not worth much more than they?[45] (Matthew 6:26) Notice Jesus relates the Father's generosity directly to the great value we are to Him, not to what we do for Him. It is through planting doubts about our identity in and our value to the Father that the enemy tries to bring the church down from living by revelation to living by natural thinking, from the liberty of the Spirit into the small-mindedness of legalism (1 Corinthians 3:1–4, Colossians 3:2, Ephesians 4:22–24). This is what Satan attempted to do with Jesus when he questioned Jesus's identity after forty days in the wilderness. "Now when the tempter came to Him, he said, 'If You are the Son of God, command that these stones become bread'" (Matthew 4:3). Notice how the enemy did not use the same name for Jesus that His Father had used at Jesus's baptism in the Jordan. To the Father, Jesus was "My *beloved* Son, in whom I am well pleased" (Matthew 3:17, emphasis added). This was spoken over Jesus before He had done any miracles or apparently achieved anything to accomplish His mission. In addressing Jesus, Satan dropped the word "beloved," and only spoke of what Jesus should do in order to prove His sonship (Luke 4:3). He had already convinced the first Adam that God was withholding Himself from him and that he had to "do" to become like God (Genesis 3:4–5). But Jesus, the last Adam (1 Corinthians 15:45), being full of the Holy Spirit, had already been rooted and established in the love of the Father and knew that there was nothing He had to do either to convince Himself of His sonship, or to move His Father to give to Him (John 2:24–25, 13:3–4). Through the

---

[45] New American Standard Version.

Father's words to Him, He had everything He needed and so do we (Luke 4:4). God doesn't need our help to be a good Father. He has been supplying all that we need from the beginning of eternity (2 Timothy 1:9), and Christ's life, death, and resurrection were the revelation of this truth; that God is a father of unlimited generosity (John 1:18, 3:16).

Chapter 13

Grace—the way home to the Father

"And he said to him, 'Son, you are always with me, and all that I have is yours'."

Luke 15:31

The work of the Holy Spirit in the church is to grow the church in the revelation of the character of the Father, revealed perfectly through Christ (1 Corinthians 2:12, Romans 8:15). The apostle Paul referred to this as being rooted and established in the love of God. When believers have not been established in the message of reconciliation and the truth that God is no longer counting their sins against them, they can't help but count their sins against themselves all the time! They effectively live as if the blood of Jesus is no more powerful than that of bulls and goats, for they live continually conscious of their sins, as if their sins have not been taken away (Hebrews 10:1–4). They live as natural men and as such they consider the idea that God is not counting their sins against them as foolishness and scandalous. The idea that sin is something that needs to be fought against and preached against at every opportunity is such a sacred cow to the natural religious mind, that the gospel, which declares that sin has been dealt with by one sacrifice forever, is continually watered down to make it palatable to the natural mind. Rather than saying "Yes and Amen" (2 Corinthians 1:20) to all God's promises being fulfilled in Christ, the modern church says "Yes and but!" This is because there is a widespread fear in the church that, unless we keep emphasizing to Christians the power of sin, they may succumb to its allure. Despite the clear teaching of scripture that He who is in us is greater than he who is in the world (1 John 4:4) and that the power of grace trumps the power of sin (Romans 5:20), Christians who have not been rooted and established in the reality of Christ's victorious life within them—the reality of the Spirit (Ephesians 3:17–19)—continue to live by what they see in the natural realm. They see the darkness of sin all around besieging the church and threatening to overwhelm us. The Spirit comes to open our eyes to see that the power of sin has been encompassed and overwhelmed by the power of God's grace (2 Kings 6:17).

There is no harm in preaching a message that lifts up the power of sin, as long as our message always lifts the power of the cross higher, for the blood of Jesus cannot be compared to that of bulls and goats (Hebrews 10:1–4). No matter how passionately people are exhorted to prune back sin in their lives, pruning back a thorn bush will never turn it into a fig tree! God's solution to our sin problem is not about pruning branches, but replacing the very root of our lives (Ezekiel 11:19, Matthew 23:25). The most effective way to strengthen believers has never been continually to direct their gaze to sin, but to their Savior, for Christ in us is our victory, not our pruning skills! (2 Corinthians 3:18, 4:6, Hebrews 12:2)

The gospel of grace—the revelation that Christ has done all that needs to be done for me to have what I need, in the hour that I need it—is like the sound of music and dancing. It is the sound of the Father rejoicing that what was lost has been restored (Luke 15:25). The gospel is the good news of what God has freely given to man. It is a message entirely about His work, not ours, and so entirely glorifies Him as the source of everything good in life (James 1:17).

Where religion demands righteousness, holiness, and a life worthy of redemption, the gospel declares that Christ "has become for us…our righteousness, holiness and redemption"[46] (1 Corinthians 1:30). This is God's wisdom; that you receive from Him freely, that you may enter into His joy, the knowledge that this is who He is: the God who loves freely. Jesus's revelatory teaching on the true nature of the Father in Luke 15 consists of three parables: the Lost Sheep, the Lost Coin, and the Lost Son. Yet each one ends with this same exhortation from the one who has found what was lost; "Rejoice with me!" (Luke 15:6, 9, 28) Can you hear the Father's invitation to the victory that Christ has won for us? To the world He cries, "Rejoice with me, agree with me, join me in the truth; that what was lost to me has been restored." This is how we live in victory over this world and the evil one; by receiving the revelation of heaven that Christ has won and we are His trophy (John 16:33). This is how the church grows up into her true identity and into the fullness of sonship; by seeing that there is nothing left for her to do but enter into the joy of the Father. This is the union of God and man that Jesus has accomplished. To every fiery dart of the enemy that cries, "What will you do for God?" our response is Jesus's victory cry from the cross; "It is finished!" (John 19:30) The only work of the believer is to believe in Christ's finished work (John 6:29).

The believer who accepts this revelation of the Spirit—this invitation from the Father to lay down his strategies and tactics to achieve blessing and simply enter into the Father's victory party—has been freed from self, for he no longer lives as if God or His blessings were something separate from him. He can now say with the apostle Paul that his experience in this life has become that "I am crucified with Christ: nevertheless I live; yet not I (ego), but Christ liveth in me: and the life which I now live in the flesh I live by the faith of the Son

---

[46] New International Version.

of God, who loved me, and gave himself for me"[47] (Galatians 2:20). Notice a mature believer's faith has moved entirely off himself and onto Christ and the sign of this is that his faith is entirely in what has already happened (He loved me and gave Himself for me) and no longer in what may happen if I sow correctly!

Notice also that the "I" which no longer lives is the "ego." This is how Jesus's story of the prodigal son finishes, with the Father asking the elder brother to leave his ego in the fields, humble himself and enter into the joy of union (Luke 15:28). This entreating of the church to leave the rags of self-righteousness behind and put on the garment of Christ's righteousness continues through the ministry of the Holy Spirit today. He directs believers to be renewed in their thinking, not to remain alienated from the life of God through a heart hardened by pride (Ephesians 4:17–24).

Yet this gospel of grace continues to be an offense and a stumbling block to many in the church. Many of us are elder brothers who have worked in the fields of religion for years and quietly wondered why the Father has apparently not celebrated our piety. Like the sound of music and dancing carried in the wind, from time to time we would become aware that "abundant life" must be more than "church life," but nothing could draw us out of the field, for that field we were working in was our life's work and had become our hope. For such a man to submit to Christ's work as his hope and his life, the revelation that hope in himself is no hope at all has to come first. It was only when the prodigal son had given up hope in his own life that he remembered the life of His Father and drew near Him (Luke 15:14–17). Even then he still struggled to give up all hope in himself and planned to work for his food as a servant (Luke 15:19), but the Father refused to receive him on any other grounds but as a much-loved son. He refused to allow him even to entertain the idea

---

[47] King James Version.

that he could contribute anything to his restoration. He insisted that love must be freely given and freely received, for anything less is not the truth of who He is; the Father who has always freely given. To enter into the joy of his Father, the younger son was only required to do one thing: to humble himself and give up the idea that he could be the source of his own salvation, and to accept freely the life his Father offered; the life of one who knows who his real source is and always will be. This is the life of a son and this revelation of sonship is what the Holy Spirit entreats the church to receive. It requires the ego; the self-life; the life that says "but what about all that I have done compared to them" to be left outside if we are to enter into the joy of the Father and the fullness of His life. Grace flows to the humble but the proud oppose it.

What does it look like to see by the Spirit; to see what the Spirit sees? What does the life look like of a person who is utterly confident that they have and always will have everything they need each day to do the will of God to be content? What does it look like when someone can see past the facts and see the truth? That life looks like the life of Jesus.

Sadly, for many Christians who have not grown up into the life of the Spirit, the facts have been the truth that we have largely lived our lives from. Yet all through the Bible, God's people are told that the facts are not *the* truth that we are to live from. We are to live from the truth the Spirit declares and reveals. In Numbers 13, twelve spies were sent into Canaan. They came back with a report on the facts. They gave the facts: there were giants living in the land and large fortified cities that looked impossible to defeat. There is nothing wrong with facing the facts, but as believers, we are not called to live from there as if the natural realm is our only reality. Jesus did not say, "You shall know the facts and the facts will set you free." He said that we would be people who know the truth and the truth would set us free (John 8:32) and He declared Himself to be this truth; Emmanuel, God with us. This was the truth that God's people have always been called to live from; God is with us (Matthew 1:23). Ten spies lived by the reality of the natural realm, but two lived by the reality of the Spirit. By the Spirit, Joshua and Caleb could see that victory was already theirs because, facts or no facts, God is with us (Numbers 14:24). We, too, are to be people of a different spirit. "What we have received is not the spirit of the world, but the Spirit who is from God, so that we may understand what God has freely given us"[48] (1 Corinthians 2:12).

This is what the gospel reveals to mankind: that the generosity of God is beyond anything the human mind can fathom, for how can we fathom the enormity of the gifts the Father has freely given us—His Son and His Holy Spirit?

Only by the revelation of His Holy Spirit can the enormity of what we have in Christ be known and received. To talk in this life of having already received all we will ever need, as if we are already forgiven and healed, makes absolutely no sense to the natural mind, which only sees this world through the natural senses. To live only by our natural senses is to live only seeing what we appear not to have. It is to live feeling constantly thirsty, but never satisfied; constantly lacking, but never full. This is the world we live in; the world of the consumer; a thirsty world, consumed with consuming. Yet Jesus told a thirsty woman once that if she drank the water He would give—His Holy Spirit—she would never be thirsty again (John 4:14).

The apostle Paul famously told the Corinthians that they were not called to live as mere men (1 Corinthians 3:3). God does not give His Spirit to men and women so that they would live and speak as mere thirsty men, but so that they could see what He sees and speak what He speaks (Colossians 4:6). In that same letter to the

---

[48] New International Version.

Corinthians, Paul described Christians as those who "have received, not the spirit of the world, but the Spirit who is from God, that we might know the things that have been freely given to us by God" (1 Corinthians 2:12).

If we do not see how much has already been freely given to us, we condemn ourselves us to a life of grasping for things we think we don't have. We grasp for love, wealth, and significance, and people around us get pushed aside or hurt by our grasping. The whole world is in turmoil through the grasping of men, who cannot see beyond the natural realm and so cannot see what God has already given; that in Christ He has given us everything He has, which is everything we need (2 Corinthians 4:4).

Jesus said that to receive His Spirit—His living water—would satisfy our thirst forever (John 4:14). Such words make no sense to the natural mind, yet when Paul heard from Corinth that the early church was beginning to grasp for power and to divide around personalities, he insisted on writing to them these words:

> "Therefore let no one boast in men. For all things are yours: whether Paul or Apollos or Cephas, or the world or life or death, or things present or things to come—all are yours. And you are Christ's, and Christ is God's." (1 Corinthians 3:21–23)

What a revelation that in Christ, all things belong to us, that indeed the same spirit that raised Christ from the dead now lives in every believer and is able to quicken or bring life to our mortal bodies, like a fountain can bring life to a desert (John 4:14, Romans 8:11). With such a revelation we can begin to live without grasping. We can live knowing that in Christ, all things are already ours, so no one can really take anything from us. Instead of grasping for things, we can start to let go of things, understanding now what

Jesus meant when He said that a man's life does not consist in the abundance of possessions (Luke 12:15). Instead of grasping onto hurt and bitterness, we can let go of those things too and forgive people as we come to see how much we have been forgiven and let go (Luke 7:47). At the end of the day, our lives will be seen most clearly, not through the things we have grasped to ourselves, but in the things we have let go of and given away freely.

The more they took from Jesus, the more obvious it became that no one was taking anything from Him, but rather that He was freely giving His life away. Pontius Pilate recognized this as Jesus stood before him. Before him stood a man, stripped and beaten, who was not pleading or grasping for life, but standing silently in full assurance that He needed nothing from Pilate, for there was nothing this world could give Him that He did not already own. This world was not going to take Jesus's life from Him, for He loved this world so much that He had already decided long ago to give His life to this world, before they ever tried to take it from Him (John 19:10–11, 1 Peter 1:20).

Seeing by the Spirit, we can see that God's mind is made up forever about us and Jesus is the revelation that God's intention was always to share everything He had with us (Romans 8:32). One day all the facts that men live from will fade away, as shadows before the rising sun. For Christians, that day has already come, for our Savior lives in us. So let us arise, church, and outshine the facts, for the light of the Holy Spirit is here, in us, that we may see and understand the things He has freely given us.

Chapter 14

The bride awakes

> "Therefore, my brethren, you also have become dead to the law through the body of Christ, that you may be married to another—to Him who was raised from the dead, that we should bear fruit to God."
>
> Romans 7:4

How do you think a husband would feel if he discovered that, after marrying the love of his life, his wife acted as if they weren't married at all and went out with other men? How would he feel if, on questioning her, he found her to be so deeply insecure about his love for her, and feeling so unworthy to be loved, that in her heart she believed he could not really have been serious in his marriage to her and that their marriage was in name only? You might think that a ridiculous scenario. No one is going to get married and then live as if the marriage isn't real. You think so? Let's have another look at many of us in the church.

For years, how many of us have struggled to rest in the love of God and believe that His love for us is the last word on our identity and destiny? How many of us have repeatedly fallen back to believing that there must be something we need to do in order to be, or stay, worthy of His life and union with Him? How many of us would confess to feeling that we must be a disappointment to God, that He may love us, but He probably doesn't like us? How much of our Christian lives have been spent asking God what He wants us to do and then worrying that we haven't done what He wanted us to?

The gospel declares that the union He offers us is based entirely on Christ's obedience and life (Romans 5:19, Hebrews 10:14), and that our identity is hidden in Him. Yet our striving to please God, the widespread lack of fulfillment that drives believers to seek continually something "new," and the ease with which we pass judgment on others, all reveal that for many of us, our hope is more on ourselves and our work for Him rather than on Christ and Him crucified. So many of us take this gift of union with Him—the gift of His life, the Christ life, the sinless life, what Romans 7:4 calls the "married" life—and we mix it with our old "apart from Him" life, our old "If I try harder I will get more and do better" life. The result is that we get something that has the outward appearance of holiness and godliness, but somehow lacks the power, the joy, the liberty, and the abundant generosity of Christ's life (1 Corinthians 13:1).

Romans 7:4 declares the reason why Christ gave His body for us. It was so "that we would be married to another." We cannot be married to two different lives at the same time. We cannot live as if we are married and single at the same time. We cannot live believing that we are one with Him (1 Corinthians 6:17), blessed with every blessing He has to give (Ephesians 1:3) and at the same time believe that He has not yet given us everything He has to give, but could be persuaded to pour out more if we pray hard enough! Yet that very double-mindedness is where many of us have lived for years and the result is that we struggle to receive the grace of God. James warned us of the result of living double-mindedly about the truth of God's generosity to give freely, to give without finding fault:

"If any of you lacks wisdom, let him ask of God, who gives to all liberally and without reproach, and it will be given to him. But let him ask in faith, with no doubting, for he who doubts is like a wave of the sea driven and tossed by the wind. For let not that man suppose that he will receive anything from the Lord; he is a double-minded man, unstable in all his ways." (James 1:5–8)

Now look once more at Romans 7:4. "Therefore, my brethren, you also have become dead to the law through the body of Christ, that you may be married to another." Can you see it? God sees you as married to Christ. He took your old life, your old, single life where you were separated from God in your sin, onto Himself on the cross and He killed and buried it, so that anyone who receives the gift of faith from God can live in a new state and reality before God, a new state of being that the Bible calls being "in Christ." The Holy Spirit's work is to declare this new state into the souls of men and women, that they would *be* whom God knows them and sees them to *be*; married to Him.

The final part of this verse names the evidence of this union: "…that you may be married to another—to Him who was raised from the dead, that we should bear fruit to God." Without remaining in this reality and believing in the power of His grace toward us and in us; without remaining in the truth that His Spirit and our spirits are one, we can bear no fruit! Jesus declared that branches cannot bear fruit if they attempt to live apart from their vine (John 15:5). The fruit that we bear when we believe that God has so comprehensively dealt with our sin that we are now dead to sin and are joined in our spirits with His sinless life, is listed in Galatians 5:22–23 and includes love, joy, peace, and patience. In other words, the result of renewing our minds to our new married state is that we start to appear like the one our heart and minds are married to: Christ.

This is the perfecting work of the Holy Spirit, who only ever addresses believers according to their new state; that is according to who they now are in the Spirit. The Holy Spirit deals with us according to the reality He knows, not according to how we feel. He speaks to us as a new man in Christ. He does not speak to us according to who we think we are; a poor sinner trying their best for God. He only speaks to us as who Christ declares we are; a totally new creation, joined to the Lord and one spirit with Him (1 Corinthians 6:17). The Holy Spirit does not minister to your idea of you (poor me, a long way from God, struggling in sin), for in His reality that person does not exist. You may not reckon that "self" to be dead, but the Holy Spirit does, or He would not have authored Romans 6:11 ("reckon yourselves to be dead indeed to sin"). You may only see yourself in the natural realm and see the sin in your life, but the Holy Spirit sees by God's reality. He sees your sin where God put it; on Christ's body on the cross and then dead and buried. He knows that through Christ's body the old sinner was put to death (Romans 6:4). He knows He can be of no help to you by speaking to you as if that person still lives (Ephesians 4:22–24). The Holy Spirit only ministers to one person, you in Christ, not to two people. Jesus confirmed that we are made perfect, not in two, but in one! (John 17:23)

The world's system values people according to what they can do. God does not value us according to what we can do for Him. The cross set us free from that system because it declared our true value to God: Christ. Religion that exhorts us to do more for God is a product of the spirit of this world. The gospel does not say "do," it says "be" (2 Corinthians 5:20). All the "doing" was done by Christ in order that we would be who He has made us to be: one with Him. That is not to say there is not much to be done in this world, but it is to be done *of* Him and not merely *for* Him. You can be sure the day Jesus visited Martha and Mary that Mary too worked hard, but her work began and emerged out of her rest with Christ. Martha's focus was on impressing Jesus. Mary's was on being impressed by

Jesus. Indeed there is much work to be done to share the message of the gospel in our community, but if we do not start from a place of revelation of our true state before God, we will only lead them into church life rather than a Christ life.

Christ did not shed His blood to give us a life of feeling insufficient, incomplete, never good enough, never ready, or a life living according to the natural senses. If I do not allow the gospel of the grace of God and the Holy Spirit to change my mind (*metanoia*, true repentance), so that I no longer live as if my sin separates me from God, then I will live as if my sin separates me from God! I will live a merely religious life of doubt and fear, where my heart constantly cries to God, "Is this enough yet?" I will live as "ever the bridesmaid but never the bride," always waiting for a better day, but never living in the better day or bearing the fruit of my union with Him, because my mind has never been renewed to the truth that from the cross, God has already declared "It is enough!" The apostle Peter confirmed that the reason believers fail to grow in Christ is that they have not been rooted and grounded in the reality of their true state before God. "For he who lacks these things is short-sighted, even to blindness, and has forgotten that he was cleansed from his old sins" (2 Peter 1:9).

Believer, you are married to Christ. Let us stop examining our lives from a merely natural point of view and behaving like men (1 Corinthians 3:3). Let us allow the Holy Spirit to speak to us as those hidden in Christ and married to Him. Let His words wake us up to Christ in us, for if we don't see Christ in ourselves, how can we expect the world to? (John 17:22–23). This question of our identity—who we believe ourselves to be—is addressed consistently throughout the New Testament as we are exhorted to be, today, before the world, whom God has redeemed us to be.

> "Therefore, we are ambassadors for Christ, as though God were making an appeal through us; we beg you on behalf of Christ, be reconciled to God. He made Him who knew no sin to be sin on our behalf, so that we might become the righteousness of God in Him. And working together with Him, we also urge you not to receive the grace of God in vain—for He says, 'At the acceptable time I listened to you. And on the day of salvation I helped you.' Behold, now is 'the acceptable time,' behold, now is 'the day of salvation'."[49] (2 Corinthians 5:20–6:2)

Years ago, my father had the family business attached to our home. He was a vet and he was always very busy and frequently running late to start his surgery, so the waiting room attached to our kitchen was usually full of people who had been waiting for a long time for their turn to see him. It often gave me such delight to enter that waiting room and know that everyone expected me, as the last one in, to sit quietly and wait my turn, and instead I would walk past them all and go straight in to speak with my father.

With my earthly father, I never joined a queue to see him. But my heavenly Father was a different story. For years that is where a religious mind-set—a mind in which my hope of God's blessing was dependent on my holiness, my obedience, or my faith—kept me; in a queue. I was forever waiting for God to get around to my case. I believed that my waiting was what would earn me God's attention and favor. I imagined my requests to God working their way slowly up to the top of His list, until one day He decides that I have suffered enough waiting to deserve an answer and on that day He relents and answers my prayer. That seemed quite a reasonable way to think at the time, after all, who was I to think that I was anyone special. I was

---

[49] New American Standard Bible.

just one among millions sitting in the queue in God's waiting room. It seemed to me that I was being very humble by quietly waiting my turn, and that I was demonstrating faith by believing that God would one day answer my prayers.

By the grace of God, through the revelation of His Word and His Spirit, I can now see what I could not see before.

1. Offering my waiting or my suffering (or my faith or my obedience or my prayers or my anything!) as the reason God should bless me, I am living with faith in myself, not in Christ (Ephesians 2:8).

2. To ensure that no man could ever diminish the love of God (*agape*) (Strong's G26) by bringing it down to man's level (which is conditional love), God gave us everything He had to give to us, at just the right time, before we had done anything to deserve it (Romans 5:8, 8:32, Ephesians 1:3).

3. To try and move God to give me something He has already given me is an exercise in futility and unbelief in the finished work of Christ (Hebrews 10:11–22, especially v.18, Romans 10:1–4).

4. If even my own father did not require me to join a waiting line to see Him, how much more does my Father in heaven entreat me to come boldly before Him! (Matthew 7:11, Hebrews 10:19–22)

The greatest price in history was paid to restore us into fellowship with God: the blood of Jesus. Only unbelief would cause a man to try and add his own works (patience, prayers, faith, suffering) onto Christ's work. To the natural mind it seems like an eminently reasonable thing to do to offer God our best efforts as the reason He should bless us, and because much of the church has never grown up out of natural thinking, such offerings have become commonplace and acceptable. So every year someone will bring out a new teaching claiming that if only you pray this prayer so many times a day, or give this amount of money to this particular cause, or if only you understood the cycle of the moons, or gave certain offerings on certain Jewish feast days, then the blessing of God would be yours. Someone else says, "No. I have discovered that what we need to do is to pray longer and harder and then God will release His blessing and, by the way, I have written a book naming the correct prayers!" Another claims, "No. We are singing the wrong songs. If only you bought my album and sung these songs instead, God would release His blessing!"

The only problem is that to believe that you need to do something more to make yourself acceptable enough to God so that He will "pour out His Spirit," you will first have to deny that you are now living in the "acceptable day" of the Lord. You will have to deny that anyone who is in Christ has been made "accepted in the beloved" (Ephesians 1:6).

Every minister of the gospel has a responsibility to preach the gospel of Christ, not the gospel of the Galatians, in order that believers would grow up into one new man in Christ (Ephesians 4:15). The Holy Spirit is still urging His body, the church, not to receive the grace of God in vain, but to believe that "at the acceptable time I listened to you and on the day of salvation I helped you"[50] (2 Corinthians 6:2). Church, behold the truth and be transformed in your thinking. "Now is the acceptable time. Now is the day of salvation" (2 Corinthians 6:2). No more waiting for revival to be poured out. The reviver was poured into your spirit the hour you believed, as you received Him, so walk in Him (Colossians 2:6). We have everything we need today to live in the blessing of God. All

---

[50] New American Standard Bible.

we need to do is awaken our souls to the glorious truth and for this we have the glorious gospel, which is the voice of God, to waken the dead, and the light of God that pierces the darkness of natural thinking. This is why we need only preach what Christ has done for man and not what man should do for Christ, for we are only transformed into His likeness by beholding Christ's finished work (Romans 12:2). It is the light of the sun that germinates the seed, so let no man slip your performance between you and the Son and slip you back into the shadowland of religion. Stop sitting in a religious queue. He has shone His light in our spirits so that we may arise to walk as one resurrected, alive to God, and dead to sin. We can walk boldly through this life, confident and freed from anxiety, because all our confidence is now in His life *in* us and not in our life *for* Him.

The apostle Paul knew that if people could see what Christ had done for them on the cross, their eyes would open and they would see themselves and this world through new eyes; God's eyes (2 Corinthians 5:16). So of all the things he could preach to people, he was determined to preach this one thing above all: Christ and Him crucified (1 Corinthians 1:23, 2:2).

He knew that if people began to see that He who knew no sin was made sin on the cross for them so that they could become the righteousness of God in Christ Jesus (2 Corinthians 5:21), if they began to see that the abundant provision of God's grace included the gift of His righteousness (Romans 5:17), then they could begin to see that God is now able to freely commune with them and live in them, so that in Him they now lack no good thing (1 Corinthians 3:16). When a man believes he lacks no good thing from God, he has made the greatest gain in all of creation; he has been restored to communion with His creator. He has contentment and godliness, and all this by the grace of God (1 Timothy 6:6). Now the life he lives is the risen life, for his thinking has risen out of the natural realm and into the heavenly one, into the mind of Christ. Now the prayers he prays glorify God, because they are not just prayers that rise to heaven; they are prayers that come from heaven.

A mature church is a church that looks like Christ. One of Jesus's last acts was to demonstrate maturity to His disciples by kneeling to wash their feet. John's Gospel describes Jesus rising to serve. This is the mark of maturity in Christ's disciples: they rise in order to serve, and John 13:3–4 records the revelation that Jesus carried that enabled Him to rise:

> "Jesus, knowing that the Father had given all things into His hands, and that He had come from God and was going to God, rose from supper and laid aside His garments, took a towel and girded Himself."[51]

Here we see the revelation that the Holy Spirit imparts to the body of Christ, to enable them to rise out of mere "church life" and into "Christ life" (Ephesians 4:15). It is the revelation of our identity and our destiny, and both are Christ. He is the revelation of where we came from and where we are going. It is the revelation that Christ promised; that we are not orphans, but children of a good heavenly Father (John 14:18). Christ is our author and finisher, our Alpha and Omega. It is not our job to finish what He started. He will complete the good work He began in us (Philippians 1:6). Let us allow the Holy Spirit to so persuade us of this truth that we effectively live as if it is already done, as if "as He is, so also are we in this world"[52] (1 John 4:17). This is where heaven lives: in the light of the finished work. This is the heavenly light that the gospel of grace shines into this world and by it the bride of Christ awakens and rises to live the life she was destined for: Christ's life.

---

[51] New American Standard Bible.
[52] New American Standard Bible.

Chapter 15

A finished work, an ascended church

> "Jesus, knowing that the Father had given all things into His hands, and that He had come from God and was going to God, rose from supper and laid aside His garments, took a towel and girded Himself."
>
> John 13:3–4

For many years, I believed that for God to be good to me and for my prayers to be answered, then I needed to start ticking more boxes on the list I kept hearing about; the list of things that the church told me I needed to be doing for God. It was a list that never seemed to end, because when you preach the gospel of the unfinished work (religion), nothing ever seems to get finished. In fact the gospel of the unfinished work does actually finish something. For multitudes of people, it has finished them with church and with God. Their patience is finished. They are finished with waiting around for God to do something and being told time and again that He couldn't do it because they hadn't prayed well enough or lived well enough.

This misunderstanding that we are saved by grace, but kept saved by our performance, explains why many Christians see the gospel message of grace as an elementary teaching, something we need to teach the world, whereas we in the church need to move on to something "deeper." In attempting to go deeper, we get caught up in all sorts of teachings that sound very important and impressive. It may take years for us to notice that by leaving behind the simplicity of the gospel of grace, we have cut ourselves off from the power to live the Christian life (2 Corinthians 11:3). We are left listening longingly to the testimonies of new believers and wondering what happened to the joy of our own salvation!

For over 25 years I have been telling my wife, Nicola, "I love you." I have yet to hear her say, "That's all you ever say, Can't I have a more varied diet? Isn't it time you changed the message and moved on to something deeper?" The gift of grace from Christ is the Father's declaration of love to us (John 3:16). Is it possible to get too much grace? You can only believe it is if you believe it is possible to get too much of Christ or too much of the love of the Father. I believe that preaching and teaching continually that the Christ life is a gift of love and grace, and not a religious reward, brings unbelievers to faith and restores to believers the joy of their salvation. This is the joy of knowing that—despite what many may have told them—their Father is *not* withholding Himself from them until they do better, but has already freely given them all that He has in Christ (Luke 15:31). That joy is our strength and so a diet of the gospel of grace is the richest soul food a believer can receive. The gospel is a "grace greenhouse" and, under its light and protection, people who have struggled to grow in the chilly atmosphere of religion thrive and blossom.

On the day each of us became a Christian, a party started in heaven (Luke 15:7). We may have lost the excitement of the joy of our salvation, but heaven has not. I don't think we had permission to leave the party, to get past what God has done for us, and to make our salvation about what we have done for Him. The Holy Spirit is inviting us back into the party that is grace, the revelation that we are His sons, not His servants (Luke 15:28–32), for only in the acknowledgment of the good things we already have is our faith made effective (Philippians 1:6). There is a river of life beginning to flow in power across the nations, as more and more believers repent of waiting for God to pour out again His Spirit from above and instead receive the truth that those rivers flow from our innermost bellies because that is where the same Spirit that rose Christ from the dead now lives (Romans 8:11). Waves of mercy and waves of grace will flow from His church as He always intended (John 7:38). Only when we know what we already have will we stop living as if we don't have it. We have the love and favor of God on and in our lives, for our sin has been completely dealt with (2 Corinthians 5:21) and the degree to which the church will awaken to this truth is the degree to which the nation will awaken to Christ and His church in its midst. The hour the church understands what it is to receive freely the power of His Spirit is the hour she begins to give freely the power of His Spirit. The hour the church will believe that our waiting is over and that at just the right time He has already heard us and helped us is the hour we will declare to the world with authority, "Indeed, the 'right time' is now. Today is the day of salvation!" (2 Corinthians 6:2)

The song the Holy Spirit has been singing over me and in me is the song of the happy Father. The same words of this heavenly love song are repeated in each of the three parables of Luke 15: the Lost Coin, the Lost Sheep and the Lost Son. Three times we hear this heavenly refrain, "Rejoice with me."

I believe this is the song of the Father, sung by the Holy Spirit over the church. Through this love song, He calls back His church, estranged in the fields of religion by her own efforts, to enter into the joy of His finished work, the joy of union with Christ. To an elder brother church, sin-conscious and self-conscious, He is still declaring the same truth that the father spoke to his elder son; "Son, you are always with me, and all that I have is yours." This truth that all the Father has is already given to us in Christ, is the truth that ascends the church out of the natural soulish realm and into the supernatural life of the Spirit, out of striving to move God and into rest; His rest over His finished work. It cuts the root of religion like an ax and sets us free to rise up and live from a heavenly perspective and in the joy of heaven over Christ's finished work. It roots and establishes us in the love of God and in our eternal identity in the Son, for, as Christ showed us at the last supper, only those who know their origin and their destiny have the grace to rise and serve selflessly (John 13:3–5).

This rising of the church happens through the revelation of the Spirit, so that we can see from, live from, worship from, and pray from a higher place, from a heavenly perspective. God has a heavenly vision *for* us and it is nothing less than His heavenly vision *of* us. Religion wraps us up in ourselves, but the gospel of grace unbinds us to live and move and have our being in Him. By His grace we can begin to see that the reason He gave gifts of ascension ministries (Ephesians 4:10–15) was so that He would have an ascended people; an ascended church.

What can an ascended church see? What can we see from a heavenly perspective? When you see from heaven, you see from the finished work. You can speak as if everything that needs to be done has been done. This is always how God intended that the enemy's work on this earth would be finished, by men and women who see and speak from the heavenly realm, the realm of the finished work, the realm of the Lamb who was slain *before* the foundation of the world, the realm of the Spirit! (Matthew 16:16–17)

Only the gospel of the finished work will finish the enemy, for in the light of what God has done, the enemy is finished. Wherever the light of the kingdom of heaven comes, the kingdom of darkness is finished, for in light of the truth of God's generosity in Christ, no lie can remain (John 8:32). So let the light shine, the light of what Christ has done. Jesus Christ has defeated sin and sickness and those who live from that message are the light of the world (Matthew 5:14). Let us preach the full light of the gospel, not the half-light of religion, for the nations have sat in the shadows for long enough. It is God's will that it would also be said of this generation, "The people who have sat in darkness have seen a great light." Religion has been the hope of the nations for too long. Now let us preach Christ alone, as the hope of the nations, by declaring the gospel undiluted, unleavened, and unshackled from man's performance. We have seen what religion; the gospel of the unfinished work can do. Now let us see what the gospel of the finished work can do. Let us eat and drink of His Word over us; "complete in Christ" (Colossians 2:10). Let us be filled with the joy of the Spirit over how completely Christ has saved us. Let the nations see our joy and ask us for the food that brings it and let us tell them that the fullness they see is His fullness that we have all received and grace for grace (John 1:16). Let us allow the gospel of His grace to unbind our hearts, which have been wrapped up for too long in our religious performance. Let the church begin to radiate the joy of heaven, the joy of the Father over His children restored. Let the sound of music and dancing, the sound of victory, and the sound of heaven rise up in the church so that this generation looks up to see Christ in us and the Father it never knew.